Irish
Cookbook

Nuala Cullen

Gill & Macmillan

Gill & Macmillan Ltd
Hume Avenue, Park West
Dublin 12
with associated companies throughout the world
www.gillmacmillan.ie

© 2005 Nuala Cullen

0 7171 3616 7

Index compiled by Cover to Cover
Illustrations by Kate Walsh
Design by Slick Fish Design
Print origination by Carole Lynch
Printed in Malaysia

This book is typeset in 9/14 pt Avenir.

A catalogue record for this book is available
from the British Library.

1 3 5 4 2

Contents

Introduction

There is an elemental pleasure in cooking with eggs: they taste so good and cook so quickly and not only are they an essential ingredient in all kinds of baking and desserts, their unique versatility means they can be eaten at any time of the day.

Many people recall with nostalgic pleasure the childhood breakfasts of buttery soft-boiled eggs broken into a warmed bowl and served with those fingers of buttered toast known to generations of children as 'soldiers'. Drinks such as eggflips (similar to the popular American eggnog) made from eggs whipped with hot milk, a pinch of nutmeg and sugar, and sometimes a spoonful of sherry or brandy, were an all-purpose restorative for convalescents and children. A variant was a raw egg beaten with fresh orange juice and sugar, especially good with the ubiquitous dash of sherry.

When, in the 1920s, Arnold Bennett, the novelist and drama critic, had finished his nightly theatre-going, it was his custom to take his supper at the Savoy Hotel, where his usual fare was the famous omelette created especially for him and which still bears his name today. And how right he was, for egg dishes are just the perfect thing after a tiring day. But eggs aren't just delicious to eat, they are also the cheapest form of protein available — two eggs provide a quarter of our protein needs for a day — and with only 85 calories each, even serious weight watchers can indulge themselves.

In addition to the protein, there are all the benefits of a wide range of vitamins, A, D, E and B and especially B12, which vegetarian diets can easily miss out on. A very important component of egg yolks is lecithin, vital for many of our bodies' metabolic processes, and to top it off eggs have lots of minerals such as zinc, iron, phosphorus, and selenium, that marvellous antioxidant of which we hear so much.

The egg has had an undeserved bad press in recent times, demonised, particularly in America, in the obsession with cholesterol. Now, thanks to new research, it has become clear that saturated fat in the diet, and not the cholesterol in food, has the most influence on blood cholesterol levels.

How many eggs should we eat? Current guidelines recommend that a healthy person can eat up to 7–8 eggs per week and those on a cholesterol-lowering diet 5–6 eggs a week, while the World Health Organisation advocates 10 eggs per week including those used in cooking. Raw eggs, however, are not recommended for the pregnant, the very young, or those with compromised immune systems.

To get the maximum nutrition from your eggs, try to buy the best procurable eggs from the best source you can find, keep an eye on the date stamps, and as the shells are porous, store them carefully in their boxes in the fridge. Ireland is one of only four European countries with an EU-approved plan for the prevention and control of salmonella — all egg farms are routinely tested and monitored by the Department of Agriculture and Food — so we can enjoy our eggs with confidence.

Many easily prepared homely dishes will be found in the following pages, as well as those with a more elegant twist or unusual provenance. I hope you will enjoy cooking them and discovering the particular magic of eggs.

1

Boiled Eggs and Oeufs Mollets

Boiled Eggs

'The breakfast egg is a Victorian institution; whatever else there was for breakfast — kidneys, chops, bacon, or kedgeree, with tea or coffee, marmalade or honey — there was always a meek little cluster of boiled eggs, set modestly apart upon a chased silver stand, with their spoons beside them (like St Ursula's virgins on shipboard).' Dorothy Hartley, *Food in England*

Boiling an egg is considered so simple a task that it is used as a measure of competence (or incompetence), yet there are variables even here. To achieve perfection the timing must be exact, and the egg must be fresh — and if it's free range and organic, so much the better.

To tell if an egg is fresh: (1) gently lower it into a glass of cold water. If the egg is very fresh it will sink to the bottom. As it ages it becomes more buoyant and will float to the top. (2) Crack the egg onto a plate. A very fresh egg will have two distinct layers of white, the layer surrounding the yolk being plump and high. The older the egg, the more this layer will flatten and the definition between the layers will be lost.

To boil your eggs, choose a saucepan that will just hold the eggs; too large and the eggs will bash about and crack. Bring the saucepan of water to the boil, and taking large eggs at room temperature, lower them gently into the water. Timing from the moment the water returns to the boil, cook for 5 minutes. Use a timer if you have one and keep the water at a simmer — boiling too hard toughens the egg whites. After 5 minutes the whites will be set and the yolks soft.

It is a form of heresy to suggest boiling eggs that have been taken directly from the fridge — allegedly they are more likely to crack than eggs at room temperature — though I do it every day and find that some brands of eggs crack in hot water regardless of temperature and others don't — the quality of the shell seems to be the determining factor. Eggs boiled directly from the fridge will take 6 minutes to cook.

An alternative method is to cover the eggs with cold water, bring quickly to the boil and, timing from the moment the water bubbles, cook for 5 minutes for a set yolk and white, or 4 minutes for a lightly set white. This method is accurate, but you need to stand over the pan, waiting for the moment it starts to bubble.

For eggs with very soft whites and runny yolks, known as coddled eggs and considered more digestible, put the eggs in when the water boils, cover the pan and remove it from the heat. The eggs will take from 7 to 10 minutes to cook, depending on their size.

To hard-boil eggs, cover the eggs with boiling water and, timing from the moment the water returns to the boil, simmer gently for 9–10 minutes before immediately immersing in cold water. Overcooking produces that greenish ring around the yolk, caused by chemical reactions within the egg, and though quite harmless it's the source of that sulphurous smell that many people, particularly children, find so unpleasant.

Peeling newly laid hard-boiled eggs can be tricky — the white sticks firmly to the membrane on the inside of the shell. However, this means that the eggs are truly fresh. When they are 3 or 4 days old this condition disappears. Peeling under running water helps a little.

Quails eggs: These beautiful little eggs with their pretty speckled shells are usually served hard-boiled to show off their lovely colouring, with a dish of sea salt for dipping. They take 3 minutes to hard-boil (4 minutes for the slightly larger ones). Peeled, dipped in flour, beaten eggs, breadcrumbs and deep-fried, they make great miniature Scotch eggs to serve with drinks. Alternatively, fill pastry tartlets with a purée of chicken (200 g/8 oz/2 cups cooked and seasoned chicken and a shallot, blended with 3 tablespoons of double cream) and top with one or two quails eggs.

Chinese tea eggs: Hard-boil the eggs, cool and gently crack the shells all over. Put the unpeeled eggs in boiling water to cover, add 2 tablespoons of soy sauce, 2 teaspoons of Chinese Five Spice Powder, half a teaspoon of cayenne or chilli powder and 2 tablespoons of scented Chinese tea or your favourite tea. Simmer very gently for about one and a half hours, topping up the water as it boils away. Leave in the water until quite cold before gently peeling away the shells to expose the delicate crazed pattern. Piled in a little pyramid on fresh green salad leaves they look very pretty — a useful item for the picnic basket, too.

Pickled eggs: Hard-boil the required number of eggs as described above and chill in cold water. Peel the eggs and put them in a large jar with a plastic (or plastic-lined) lid. Bring sufficient white wine vinegar to cover them to the boil with 2 teaspoons each of peppercorns and allspice berries, a piece of bruised ginger root and 1–2 cloves of garlic. Simmer for 5 minutes and when cold pour over the eggs and seal tightly. They are ready for use in a month's time and are excellent with salads and cold meats.

STUFFED EGGS

Stuffed eggs are among those ubiquitous little preparations that everybody knows how to do, thinks nothing of, and yet, like Melba Toast and Béarnaise Sauce, the leftover rate is minimal.

Boil large eggs for 9 minutes, gently turning them about once or twice, and cool in cold water. Peel and cut in two lengthways, scoop out the yolks and mash, or put through a sieve, with your chosen ingredients. The eggs can be prepared several hours in advance, covered and refrigerated.

Suggestions for fillings

- sour cream
- scallions
- Tabasco
- snipped chives
- 1 gherkin

Mash the first four ingredients to a cream with the egg yolks, season well and pipe into the egg halves. Top each with a slice of gherkin.

- anchovies
- butter
- red salmon eggs or lumpfish caviar

Rinse and dry the anchovies. Mash with the butter to make a smooth paste, pipe around the egg halves, covering the surface, and top with the caviar.

- mayonnaise
- cream or milk
- curry powder
- walnuts

Toss the walnuts in curry powder and toast lightly in a teaspoon of oil on the pan. Mash the yolks with enough mayonnaise, cream and curry powder to give a good flavour and texture, pipe or spoon into the egg halves and top each with a walnut half.

- prawns
- crème fraîche
- finely chopped and well-drained cucumber
- ¼ small red pepper
- lemon juice

Mash the yolks with the crème fraîche until smooth and beat in the finely chopped prawns and cucumber. Season well, add lemon juice to taste, pipe or spoon into the egg halves and top with very fine shreds of red pepper.

EGGS WITH TUNA SAUCE AND BARLOTTI BEANS
SERVES 4–6 AS A STARTER

- 2 x 400 g/14 oz tins Barlotti or Pinto beans, drained and rinsed
- 2 medium ripe tomatoes, skinned and seeded
- 5–6 basil leaves
- 2 tablespoons olive oil
- 2–3 spring onions
- 1–2 cloves garlic
- 1–2 tablespoons chopped chives, chervil or other herbs
- 1 tablespoon lemon juice
- 200 g/7 oz/¾ cup canned tuna in brine
- 1 carton crème fraîche
- 6 large hard-boiled eggs, sliced lengthways
- 4–5 anchovies in oil, for garnish (optional)
- salt, black pepper and cayenne pepper

Put the beans in a small bowl with the finely chopped tomatoes, basil leaves torn into small shreds, olive oil and seasoning to taste. Set aside.

Put the spring onions, garlic, half the herbs and the lemon juice into a blender and blend until smooth, adding a very little olive oil or liquid from the tuna if the mixture is difficult to work, or chop very finely by hand. Add the drained tuna and the crème fraîche and mix to a thick cream. Taste for seasoning, adding more lemon juice and cayenne pepper to taste. The texture should be like softly whipped cream.

Pour the beans onto a serving dish and arrange the eggs, cut side up, over the beans. Spoon the sauce over the eggs and leave to infuse for about 30 minutes before serving. Garnish with the anchovies cut into fine strips and scatter with the remaining herbs.

DEEP-FRIED STUFFED EGGS WITH REMOULADE SAUCE

SERVES 4 FOR LUNCH OR 8 AS A STARTER

Garnished with salad leaves and coriander or chive sprigs, these deep-fried eggs make an unusual starter or light lunch. Equally good hot or cold and easy to pack for picnics. Serve with Sauce Remoulade (page 126) on the side.

- 75 g/3 oz/½ cup chorizo or similar spicy sausage
- 4 spring onions
- 1 red chilli, seeded and cut into fine strips

- 8 large hard-boiled eggs
- 2 tablespoons finely chopped coriander or parsley
- 3 tablespoons crème fraîche or mayonnaise
- 3 tablespoons flour
- 2 beaten eggs
- 100 g/4 oz/1 cup fine dry breadcrumbs
- oil for frying
- black pepper and mace

Peel away any papery skin from the chorizo and chop with the spring onions and chilli as finely as you can — a small electric chopper is ideal.

Cut the eggs in half lengthways, carefully remove the yolks and add with the coriander to the chorizo mixture. Mash well together, adding just enough crème fraîche to give a stiff paste. Season well with black pepper and mace. It probably won't need salt.

Stuff each egg half generously with the sausage mixture. Press two halves together to re-shape the eggs, leaving a stripe of stuffing visible. Gently smooth exposed stuffing with a knife. Roll the eggs in flour, dip in the beaten eggs and finally roll gently in the breadcrumbs, repeating the egg and breadcrumb step where there are any bald spots. Leave to set for 15–20 minutes in the fridge.

Put sufficient oil to cover the eggs in a large saucepan and heat until it is hot enough to brown a cube of bread in 30 seconds. Gently lower 2 or 3 eggs at a time into the oil, turning about gently until golden brown. Drain on paper and keep warm in a low oven until all the eggs are cooked. The eggs will brown very quickly, almost before they are warmed through, and a few minutes in a low oven will do them no harm. Serve the sauce separately.

GRATIN OF EGGS WITH LEEKS
SERVES 6 AS A STARTER OR 3–4 FOR LUNCH

- 350 g/12 oz/3 cups cleaned leeks
- 75 g/3 oz/6 tablespoons butter
- 1 clove garlic, finely chopped
- 1 tablespoon each lemon juice and grated lemon rind
- 300 ml/½ pint/1¼ cups cream
- 9 large hard-boiled eggs
- 2 tablespoons grated strong Cheddar or Parmesan
- 25 g/1 oz/¼ cup breadcrumbs
- salt, black pepper and nutmeg

Slice the leeks lengthways into strips and blanch in boiling water for 3–4 minutes. Drain and blot dry with kitchen paper. Chop finely. Melt the butter in a frying pan, add the leeks, garlic and lemon rind and sauté until the leeks are soft. Pour in half the cream, adding lemon juice to taste, and stir until the mixture thickens, adding more cream until the consistency is thick but not too stiff. Season generously, adding nutmeg to taste.

Cut the shelled eggs in half lengthways and lay them, cut side up, in a buttered oven dish that will just hold them. Spoon the leek sauce over the eggs, scatter the cheese and breadcrumbs on top and dot with the remaining butter. Bake at 200°C/400°F/Gas 6 until golden brown.

For a more substantial dish spread a layer of mashed potatoes, well creamed with butter and milk, under the eggs before adding the sauce and finishing as above — great comfort food for supper or lunch.

STUFFED EGGS WITH RED PEPPERS AND WATERCRESS
SERVES 4 OR 6

The fresh colours of this simple starter give a summery feel to the dish. Choose a red pepper that is thick and shiny.

- 6 large eggs
- 100 g/4 oz/2 cups rocket or fresh spinach
- ½ tablespoon butter
- 1 large red pepper
- walnut or olive oil
- 5–6 tablespoons double cream
- 1 tablespoon chives, finely chopped
- 1 tablespoon parsley, finely chopped
- lemon juice
- 1 bunch watercress
- salt, black pepper and cayenne pepper

Hard-boil the eggs, cool and peel. Wash the rocket thoroughly, shake dry and cook for 2 minutes in the microwave or wilt on a pan with a nut of butter. Drain, squeeze out the moisture and chop finely.

Turn the grill to high. Cut the red pepper into quarters, remove the seeds and pith and put the pieces skinside up under the grill until the skin is blackened and blistered. Loosely wrap in foil until cool enough to scrape away the skin. Cut each piece lengthways into 5–6 thin strips. Toss in a little oil and set aside.

Cut the eggs in half lengthways and remove the yolks. Mash the yolks and cream together to a smooth paste before blending with the rocket, chives and seasoning, adding a few drops of lemon juice to sharpen the flavour. Fill the egg whites with the mixture, piling it up nicely and leaving the white edges exposed against the green filling.

Mix the peppers lightly with the watercress and dress with a little oil and lemon juice. Divide between the plates, arrange 2 or 3 egg halves on each and sprinkle with parsley.

EGG AND CHICKEN MOUSSE WITH OLIVE AND TOMATO SALAD
SERVES 6 AS A FIRST COURSE OR 4 FOR LUNCH

This unusual egg and chicken mousse from New Orleans makes an attractive addition to a summer buffet.

- 6 large hard-boiled eggs
- 2 large celery stalks
- 350 g/12 oz/2 cups cooked chicken
- ½ red and ½ green pepper
- 1 envelope gelatine
- 150 ml/5 fl oz/¼ pint/⅝ cup chicken stock
- 175 g/6 oz/¾ cup mayonnaise
- chilli sauce or Tabasco
- 1 tablespoon each lemon or lime rind and juice
- 150 ml/5 fl oz/¼ pint/⅝ cup lightly whipped cream
- salt and black pepper

Tomato salad

- 3–4 large ripe vine tomatoes
- a few basil leaves
- 3 tablespoons black olives
- 75 g/3 oz/½ cup lightly toasted walnuts
- a bunch watercress or a handful rocket or salad leaves
- olive oil
- vinegar

Finely chop the eggs and celery. Tear the chicken into strips and season well with salt and black pepper. Remove the seeds and white pith from the peppers and cut into fine strips about 5 cm (2 inches) long.

Dissolve the gelatine in the chicken stock, following the directions on the packet. Allow to cool a little before mixing into the mayonnaise. Add sufficient chilli sauce, lemon rind and juice to give a spicy, sharp flavour. Gently mix the chicken, vegetables and cream into the mayonnaise and finally fold in the finely chopped eggs. Rinse out a mould or soufflé dish with cold water, spoon the mixture into it, cover and leave to set in the fridge.

When ready to serve, turn out the mousse onto a large serving plate. (A few drops of cold water sprinkled on the plate first will make it easy to slide the mousse into place if it is off centre.)

To make the tomato salad, dress the salad leaves and arrange around the mousse. Slice the tomatoes and place on top of the salad leaves. Scatter the olives and walnuts over the tomatoes and finally tear the basil leaves into pieces and scatter over the dish.

Oeufs Mollets

Oeufs mollets, or mollet eggs, could be described as hard-boiled eggs with soft centres. They are a rather subtle and glamorous alternative to hard-boiled eggs with a very special place in French cookery.

Large eggs at room temperature are gently boiled for 6 minutes and immediately plunged into cold water. When quite cold the shells are very gently cracked all over with a spoon and the shell is carefully peeled away. The whites should be quite set and the yolk still soft. If not required immediately, put the eggs in a bowl of cold water in the fridge where they can be stored for 24 hours. Reheat in hot water for 1 minute when required.

MOLLET EGGS 'FINES HERBES'
FOR A FIRST COURSE SERVE 2 SMALL OR MEDIUM EGGS PER PERSON.
SERVES 4

Fresh herbs are the heart of this elegant yet simple mollet egg recipe and now that many herbs can be bought all year round it needn't be confined to summer. Use a variety of herbs, ideally including tarragon, chervil, chives and parsley.

- 8 small or medium eggs
- 75–100 g/3–4 oz/6–8 tablespoons butter
- 6 tablespoons chopped mixed herbs
- 4 triangles of buttered toast per serving
- salt, black pepper and lemon juice

Boil the eggs as described on page 4. Next put them first into cold water for a few minutes to stop the cooking, then peel, and transfer to a bowl of warm water to reheat slightly. Melt the butter in a pan large enough to hold the eggs, add two-thirds of the herbs and stir about until they begin to wilt. Add the eggs, season with a very little salt and a few grindings of black pepper and roll the eggs gently about until they are warm and the butter and herbs nicely infused, but don't allow the butter to burn.

Transfer the eggs to 4 heated plates and arrange the toast around them. Add a good squeeze of lemon juice to the pan, boil up for a moment, then pour the contents over the eggs. Scatter the remaining herbs over the plates and serve immediately.

MOLLET EGGS WITH PARMA HAM AND RED PEPPER SAUCE

SERVES 4

A light starter for 4, it can be made more substantial by using 2 small mollet eggs per person and doubling the quantity of ham and bread. Little pastry tartlet cases can be used instead of the bread.

- 4 x 7.5 cm/3 inch circles of good bread, not too thinly cut
- olive oil for brushing on
- 4 large mollet eggs (page 17)
- 4 slices Parma ham
- 1 quantity Red Pepper Sauce (page 127)
- ½ red pepper, cut in fine strips, for garnish

Cut one 2.5 cm/1 inch circle from the centre of each piece of bread, creating little depressions to hold the eggs. Brush the rings with olive oil and either toast or fry. Spread them out on a baking tray that will later fit under the grill and put in a very low oven to keep warm. Place the eggs in a bowl of warm water until warmed. Turn on the grill.

When the eggs are warm lift out carefully and blot dry with kitchen paper. Wrap a slice of ham around each egg and set on the bread circles. Spoon the Red Pepper Sauce over the eggs and flash under a hot grill for a few seconds until the sauce begins to glaze slightly. Garnish with the shreds of red pepper and serve immediately.

MOLLET EGGS IN PASTRY CASES
SERVES 6 AS A STARTER OR 4 AS A LIGHT LUNCH WITH A SALAD

The pastry cases can be made from frozen or homemade pastry. Frozen 'king size' vol-au-vent cases can also be used and tuna, shrimps or mussels can replace the salmon in this cold starter.

- 350 g/12 oz puff pastry
- 1 beaten egg
- 6 tablespoons cucumber, diced finely
- 175 g/6 oz/1 cup cooked flaked salmon
- 2 tablespoons chopped dill
- grated horseradish or horseradish sauce
- 175 g/6 oz /³⁄4 cup mayonnaise (page 123)

- 6 large mollet eggs (page 17)
- salad leaves and lemons, to garnish
- salt and cayenne pepper

To make the pastry cases, roll out the pastry 5 mm/¼ inch thick and cut out six 10 cm/4 inch squares with a cutter or sharp knife. Inside the squares, draw another square 1 cm/½ inch from the edge with the point of a knife, cutting into the pastry slightly. Brush the pastry with beaten egg and bake in a hot oven (200°C/400°F/Gas 6) for about 20 minutes until nicely crisped. When cool, remove the loose top from the centre of each case with the point of a knife and scrape out any soft dough.

Sprinkle the cucumber cubes with a little salt and leave to drain in a sieve for 20 minutes before blotting dry with kitchen paper. Mix the cucumber and salmon together in a small bowl, stir in the dill and season with a pinch of cayenne pepper. Add sufficient horseradish to the mayonnaise to give a good sharp flavour, then fold into the salmon mixture.

Spoon the fish into the pastry cases. Set a mollet egg on top of each and coat with the remaining mayonnaise. Arrange on a serving dish and garnish with salad leaves and lemon quarters.

2

Poached and Fried Eggs

Poached Eggs

Prepared even in the simplest way, poached eggs are delicate and delicious, yet suitable for more elaborate treatment without losing their charm. Truly fresh eggs are essential, however, if the eggs are to retain their compact shape.

There are several schools of thought as to the best way to poach eggs and one that can be discounted right away is the egg poacher, which produces a sort of steamed bun. Very popular with chefs is the whirlpool method, in which deep water is whirled around at great speed with a whisk and the egg dropped into the centre of the vortex, the force of the water shaping the egg into a perfect oval. The eggs are then transferred to warm water until the required numbers are poached.

A homelier, and easier, method is to fill a wide, deep sauté or frying pan with water deep enough to cover the eggs. Bring it to the boil, then reduce the heat until the water is barely simmering. Add a tablespoon of white vinegar to the water. This helps to coagulate the egg white but can be eliminated if preferred. Crack the eggs one at a time into a saucer, then slide into the barely bubbling water and allow to simmer for 1 minute, timing carefully. Now cover the pan and remove from the heat. Leave the eggs for 3 minutes — the whites should be set and the yolks still runny. If not, leave for another minute. Lift out the eggs with a perforated spoon, let the spoon sit for a moment on a wad of kitchen paper or a tea towel to drain, trim around the ragged edges and serve.

Don't try to poach more than about 4 eggs at a time. If more are called for, the cooked eggs can be kept warm in water as described above. When a large number is needed they can be kept in cold water in the fridge for 24 hours, reheating them in hot water for 1 minute when ready to serve.

POACHED EGGS WITH BROWN BUTTER SAUCE AND ASPARAGUS
SERVES 6 AS A STARTER OR 3
AS A LIGHT MEAL

This deceptively simple sauce is quick to make but must be done at the very last moment, so have everything ready before starting.

- 4–5 spears of asparagus per egg
- 6 large poached eggs (page 22)
- 175 g/6 oz/¾ cup butter
- 1 tablespoon fresh sage leaves, chopped
- 2 tablespoons lemon juice
- 3 tablespoons capers, rinsed and drained
- 2 tablespoons fresh herbs, finely chopped
- black pepper

Trim the fibrous ends from the asparagus and cook in boiling salted water for 5–8 minutes, depending on thickness, until tender but retaining a little bite. Drain and arrange on 6 heated plates. Carefully place the poached eggs, reheated if cooked earlier, on top.

Melt the butter in a small pan, add the sage and a turn or two of black pepper. Raise the heat and allow the butter to foam up. When it is just turning golden brown, but before it begins to burn, remove from the heat and allow to cool for a few moments. Add the lemon juice, 3 tablespoons of boiling water and the capers, shake the pan vigorously to emulsify the sauce and pour immediately over the eggs. Scatter the chopped herbs over the eggs and serve immediately with toasted crusty bread.

Note: If using dried sage a pinch will be enough.

COURGETTES WITH POACHED EGGS
SERVES 4 AS A STARTER OR LIGHT LUNCH
This pretty dish is easier than it sounds, looks and tastes delicious and can be partially prepared in advance.

- 25 g/1 oz butter
- 2–3 tablespoons frozen 'petits pois' peas
- 1 generous tablespoon chopped herbs such as tarragon, marjoram and chives
- 200 ml/8 fl oz/1 cup double cream
- 2 large courgettes
- 4 large poached eggs (page 22)
- 100 ml/4 fl oz/½ cup white wine
- 1 large tomato, skinned, seeded and chopped
- salt and black pepper
- dash of lemon juice
- 4 buttered ramekins or similar small oven dishes

Melt the butter in a medium frying pan and add the peas and herbs. Cook for a minute or two until the butter has melted again and the peas are cooked. Add the cream, season well and cook a moment longer.

Bring a saucepan of salted water to the boil. Using a mandoline or potato peeler, cut the courgettes into long broad strips. (Try to cut at least two perfect strips per ramekin. Broken strips can be used for filling in.) Blanch the strips in the boiling water for 1 minute, drain and dry with kitchen paper. To line the buttered ramekins, lay 1 strip across the centre, letting the ends overhang. Lay the second strip at right angles to the first, ends overhanging. Line the dish with the remaining strips until the sides are completely covered. This operation can be carried out well in advance.

Using a perforated spoon, divide the peas between the dishes and moisten with a few drops of cream. Lay the poached eggs on top, reheated if cooked earlier. Season well, then fold the courgette ends over the eggs to make tidy parcels. Keep warm. Add the wine and lemon juice to the remaining cream in the pan and boil rapidly until the sauce has reduced and thickened slightly. Stir in the chopped tomato and allow it to heat through. Turn the parcels out onto warm plates, pour the sauce over them and serve.

POACHED EGGS 'MEURETTE'
SERVES 4 AS A MAIN COURSE

Eggs are poached in red wine in this dish from Burgundy. Choose a rather light wine as it must be thoroughly reduced. Eggs Meurette are usually served as a main course but could quite easily make a starter for 8 people. The sauce, garnish and eggs can all be prepared in advance and reheated.

- 1 bottle of red Burgundy
- 300 ml/½ pint/2–3 cups strong homemade chicken stock or canned beef consommé
- 8 large eggs

Sauce

- 15 g/½ oz butter
- 1 onion, thinly sliced
- 1 carrot, thinly sliced
- 1 stick celery, thinly sliced
- 2 cloves garlic, chopped
- 1 bay leaf
- 1 sprig thyme
- ½ teaspoon black peppercorns
- 2 tablespoons each butter and flour, mashed together (beurre manie)
- 8 thick slices of bread

Garnish

- 50 g/2 oz/4 tablespoons butter
- 12 button mushrooms
- 6 shallots
- 4 slices streaky bacon

Bring the wine and stock to the boil in a large wide saucepan, reduce to a simmer and use this to poach the eggs (see page 22). Remove the eggs with a slotted spoon and set aside in a bowl of warm water. Strain any egg fragments from the poaching liquid with the slotted spoon and discard.

To make the sauce, melt the butter in a sauté pan, add the sliced onion, carrot, celery and garlic and cook slowly until the vegetables are soft but not browned. Add the vegetables and pan juices to the wine and stock mixture. Add the herbs and peppercorns and simmer gently, without a lid, until the liquid has reduced by half. Whisk the butter and flour mixture into the reduced sauce piece by piece until it is thick enough to coat the back of a spoon. Simmer for 2–3 minutes to cook the flour. Leave on the lowest possible heat to keep warm.

Meanwhile, to prepare the garnish, put half the butter in a sauté pan and cook the mushrooms and the peeled and halved shallots until tender. Push the mushroom mixture to one side, add the bacon to the pan and fry gently until crisp, then transfer with the mushroom mixture to a dish and keep warm. Don't wash the pan.

Melt the remaining butter in the pan and fry the bread on each side. Arrange 2 pieces each on heated plates. Reheat the eggs for 1 minute in hot water if cooked earlier, remove with a slotted spoon and drain on kitchen paper. Place an egg on each slice of bread, spoon the garnish on top and coat completely with the sauce.

EGGS BENEDICT

SERVES 6

Eggs Benedict has warm associations for me — it has been the family's favoured Christmas breakfast for many years and evokes all the Christmas morning kitchen aromas, wrapping paper, champagne and pleasant confusion. An American dish with its roots in France, it is simple to prepare, though, as with any dish that requires several cooking processes at once, it also needs a little co-ordination. Make the sauce first and keep warm over hot water or use the whizzed-up version on page 118 and make it ahead of time. The eggs can be poached earlier or even the night before.

- 2 slices bacon per egg
- 2 large poached eggs per person (page 22)
- ½ muffin or 1 thick round of toast per egg
- butter
- 1 quantity Hollandaise Sauce (page 116)

Grill the bacon and keep warm. Reheat the eggs for 1 minute if prepared earlier, drain and dry. Cut the muffins in two horizontally, toast and butter them. Set the muffins on a baking sheet, lay 2 slices of bacon on each, carefully set the eggs on top and spoon a generous quantity of sauce over each egg. Slide under the hot grill for a few seconds to glaze the sauce and serve immediately.

Fried Eggs

Most people have very decided views on exactly how they like their eggs fried, spurning them if they aren't just so. The few suggestions below, very tentatively offered, are for those who are still working on their fried eggs.

For fried eggs with crisped edges, heat a small heavy pan until it is quite hot and put in a tablespoon of fat — it can be butter, oil, a mixture of both, or fat saved from frying bacon. As soon as it begins to show a faint haze crack your eggs into the pan. Lower the heat immediately to avoid rubbery and indigestible whites and leave to cook for 30 seconds. If you like the yolk slightly coloured on top, tilt the pan to allow the fat to pool at one side. Spoon the fat over the eggs to lightly 'veil' the yolks, allow another 2 minutes or so to pass and your eggs are ready. Remove with a slotted egg slice, rest this on kitchen paper to absorb the surplus fat and serve.

For fried eggs without crisped edges, start with a medium hot pan, crack in your eggs and leave to cook gently for 3 minutes. Cover the pan for 2 minutes to 'veil' the yolks. Time this period carefully as the steamy heat under the lid can overcook the yolks very quickly. Remove and drain as above.

For deep-fried eggs, heat 1 cm/½ inch of oil in a deep-frying pan. When it's hot enough to crisp a piece of bread almost instantly, crack the egg carefully into the pan. Using a spoon, immediately fold the white over the yolk, making a compact shape. When the white is firm and beginning to brown, the egg is cooked. Lift out with a draining spoon and blot well on several folds of kitchen paper. Serve immediately on fried or toasted bread. It is really only possible to deep-fry eggs one at a time.

The traditional garnish is deep-fried parsley sprigs. Dip the sprigs in flour, shake off the surplus and fry them in the oil used for the eggs.

FRIED EGGS WITH ONIONS
AND SPICY LENTILS
SERVES 6

Served with a salad and plenty of good crusty bread, this little dish makes an excellent lunch.

- 1 teaspoon cumin seeds
- ½ teaspoon coriander seeds
- 350 g/12 oz/2 cups brown or Puy lentils
- 2–3 fresh red chillies, seeded and finely chopped
- 2 large ripe tomatoes, peeled, seeded and chopped
- butter and olive oil for frying
- 2 large Spanish onions, thinly sliced
- 6 large eggs
- 2 tablespoons finely chopped parsley
- salt and black pepper

Heat a small frying pan, pour in the cumin and coriander seeds and stir them about until they are nicely toasted, but don't allow them to burn.

Wash the lentils carefully and put them in a large saucepan with 1.2 litres/2 pints of water, the toasted seeds and the chopped chillies. Bring to the boil and simmer gently until the liquid is almost entirely absorbed and the lentils are tender (30–45 minutes depending on which lentils are used). If there is more than a tablespoon or two of liquid remaining at this point, drain off the surplus. Add salt and black pepper, stir in the chopped tomatoes, cover and allow to rest. Warm 6 deep plates.

Heat the olive oil in a large frying pan, add the sliced onions, cover and cook over a moderate heat until the onions have begun to soften. Turn up the heat, remove the lid and fry until they are golden brown and crisp.

While the onions are cooking, heat a 20 cm/8 inch frying pan with a lump of butter and 2 teaspoons of oil. Fry the eggs in 2 batches as directed on page*, keeping the first batch warm while frying the second. Reheat the lentils if necessary and divide between the heated plates, set the fried eggs on top and cover with the onions. Sprinkle with the parsley and serve.

HUEVOS FRITOS A LA ESPAÑOL
SERVES 4 FOR A FIRST COURSE OR
2 FOR LUNCH

The Spanish excel at frying eggs and every little *venta* in the countryside can produce at the drop of a hat perfectly fried eggs garnished with equally good fried potatoes. There are many interpretations of this popular dish, though common to all is the purée of tomatoes and red peppers. Finely chopped chorizo added to the purée gives extra flavour.

- 1 large Spanish onion
- 2 medium red peppers
- 4 large ripe tomatoes
- olive oil
- 100 g/4 oz/½ cup chorizo, finely chopped
- 2 cloves garlic, finely chopped

- 4 large eggs
- 4 thick slices of bread, toasted and cut in triangles
- salt and paprika

Peel the onion and chop finely. Cut the peppers in half, remove the seeds and pith and chop finely. Skin, seed and chop the tomatoes.

Heat 3 tablespoons of olive oil in a deep-frying pan, add the vegetables and cook very slowly, stirring from time to time, until they form a thick purée. Add the chorizo, if you are using it, and cook for a few more minutes. Season the purée with a little salt and about 2–3 teaspoons of paprika. Spread the purée in a heated serving dish and keep warm.

Wipe out the pan, heat a little more oil, fry the garlic in it for a moment, push it to the side and fry the eggs. Arrange them on top of the purée and pour the oil and garlic from the pan over the eggs. Arrange the toast triangles around the dish and serve.

FRIED EGGS WITH POLENTA AND MUSHROOMS

SERVES 6 AS A STARTER OR 3
FOR LUNCH OR SUPPER

This dish from northern Italy combines interesting flavours and textures. Both the polenta and the mushroom filling can be prepared in advance.

- 375 g/14 oz/2½ cups packet instant polenta
- 450 g/1 lb/5¼ cups mushrooms, thinly sliced
- 40 g/1½ oz/3 tablespoons butter
- 150 ml/¼ pint/¾ cup Béchamel Sauce (page 119)
- 50 g/2 oz/⅓ cup grated Parmesan
- lemon juice
- 2 tablespoons olive oil
- 6 large eggs
- 6 slices Parma ham
- Parmesan flakes, to garnish (optional)
- salt, black pepper and cayenne pepper

Make up the polenta according to the directions on the packet. While still hot, using a palette knife, spread the polenta 1 cm/½ inch thick on a buttered baking tray. Cover with clingfilm or foil to prevent a hard crust forming as it cools.

Sauté the mushrooms for about 15 minutes slowly in the butter until the moisture has evaporated and a good nutty flavour has developed. Mix the mushrooms and any pan juices with the hot Béchamel Sauce. Stir in the grated Parmesan and season generously, adding cayenne pepper and lemon juice to taste. Set aside to keep warm and wipe out the pan. Warm 6 plates and turn on the grill.

Using a biscuit cutter, cut six 7.5 cm/3 inch circles from the polenta. Heat the olive oil in the pan and fry the circles gently until hot and golden. Keep these warm while you fry the eggs.

To assemble, put the slices of polenta on a baking tray, lay a slice of Parma ham on top of each, cover with the mushroom mixture, and slide under the hot grill until the sauce starts to bubble and brown. Using an egg slice, slip the polenta circles onto the warmed plates, top each with a fried egg and serve garnished with flakes of Parmesan (peeled from a piece of Parmesan with a potato peeler).

EGGS SUR-LE-PLAT

These eggs, literally 'on a plate', are cooked in the oven in well-buttered, flat, shallow ovenproof egg dishes that hold 2 eggs. The dishes are heated in the oven (180°C/350°F/ Gas 4), 15 g/½ oz of butter is added to each and when it is melted the 2 eggs are cracked in, seasoned, and enough cream to cover the whites is poured over. (About 220 ml/ 8 fl oz/1 cup is sufficient for 4 dishes, i.e. 8 eggs.) They are returned to the oven for about 6 minutes until the whites are set but the yolks still soft. Simple and delicious, the eggs are brought directly to the table in their dishes with some good bread for mopping up. A leaf or two of fresh tarragon can be placed on each egg before the cream is added.

This simple dish is one of the basics of French egg cookery and the little oval or round metal or china oven dishes that nicely hold 2 eggs can be found in most good kitchen shops.

3

The Versatile Omelette

Almost every country in the world has its version of the omelette. It is the best of fast foods, and for the tired and hungry that seductive aroma of eggs cooking in sizzling butter can be produced in minutes, the flavour varied by an endless choice of fillings.

Omelette lovers will have their own tried and tested method and a favourite pan, too, but for those new to the subject a word on pans may be useful. Most important is the diameter of the pan. For a two or three egg French omelette, enough for one person, you need a pan with a 15 cm/6 inch base, and for this type of omelette, where the cooking has to be fast, a cheap non-stick pan is fine — it can be discarded when the lining is worn.

For frittatas and tortillas, etc., where longer, gentler cooking is needed, it's better to invest in a good quality heavier pan. Depending on how many you cook for, pans of 20 cm/8 inch to 25 cm/10 inch diameter are the most useful sizes.

A cast-iron omelette pan, kept exclusively for the purpose, used to be considered ideal, and there are excellent cast-iron pans with non-stick linings on the market. My own current favourite is a heavy aluminium pan with a non-stick lining and an enamel base. Unlined aluminium pans are good, too, but acidic ingredients must be avoided, and it is important to follow the manufacturer's directions for seasoning the pan.

Whichever pan you choose, don't put it into water while it is still hot, not even into hot water — the base will warp leaving the pan with a dome in the centre.

When it comes to cleaning, no matter what the lining, don't use an abrasive cleaner. Simply wash it with warm soapy water and dry well. If the contents have well and truly fused on, soak it in soapy water and use a soft plastic scrubber. If the pan is unlined aluminium or cast iron, rub it over with a little oil before putting it away.

The classic French omelette

If you are making omelettes for 2 or 3 people, make them individually — it's easier than juggling a large omelette and dividing it up and almost as fast. Have everything ready before you start, the table set, the plates heating, wine opened and any filling prepared. For each omelette you will need:

- 15 g/½ oz/1 tablespoon butter
- 2–3 large eggs
- 1 teaspoon oil
- salt and black pepper

Cut the butter into small cubes. Put the pan on the heat and crack the eggs into a small bowl. Gently break up the yolks and whites with a fork, stirring rather than beating, just enough to loosely blend them together — well-beaten eggs produce flat rather than puffy omelettes. Season the eggs to your taste and add half the butter cubes.

When the pan is quite hot, add the oil and the remaining butter. Increase the heat and as soon as the butter has stopped foaming, but just before it begins to brown, pour in the eggs.

Tilt the pan in all directions to spread the mixture. Allow it to stand for a few moments until the eggs begin to set around the edges, then with a fork or spoon pull the cooked area towards you to allow the liquid egg to run underneath. Repeat this until there is just a little liquid egg left on top and the omelette is ready.

Raise the handle of the pan with your left hand and flip or fold one-third of the omelette away from you, then roll onto a warm plate. Ideally, it will now be folded in three with the join underneath. The omelette should be light and puffy with a rather floppy shape and, if your pan was hot enough, have taken less than a minute from start to finish. (Chefs' lore from the days when rigorous French training ruled in professional kitchens tells how trainees were taught to make omelettes on the inner gas ring with the outer one on — the flame under the wrist — to encourage speed!)

Eat your omelette at once, as it will continue to cook in its own heat and that lovely juicy centre will be lost. A little practice will tell you how much runny egg, called *baveuse* in French cooking, to leave on top before folding. It's a matter of taste, of course, but the finished omelette must be soft and juicy.

It's always a toss-up whether an omelette is nicer plain or filled, but the filling shouldn't drown out the buttery egg taste — 1 or 2 tablespoons will be enough, warmed if necessary, and spread over the runny egg before folding.

Fillings

Fines herbes. The classic filling for a French omelette — 1 or 2 tablespoons of finely chopped fresh herbs such as parsley, chives, chervil, tarragon, etc., or whatever you please. Tarragon is rather dominant, particularly when dried, so taste carefully as you go.

Mix in two-thirds of the herbs when stirring the eggs and sprinkle the remainder over the finished omelette with a few flakes of butter.

Scallions. 3 or 4 sliced scallions softened in butter, mixed with 1 tablespoon of chopped fresh coriander and stirred into the eggs before cooking. This is truly delicious and enough for 2 omelettes.

Mushroom filling. Cook 50–75 g/2–3 oz/¾ to 1 cup of finely sliced mushrooms in a little butter until reduced and the liquid has evaporated. Season carefully with a tiny pinch of salt, plenty of fresh black pepper and a little lemon juice.

Cheese filling. 1 or 2 tablespoons of grated hard cheese, such as Parmesan or Cheddar, sprinkled over the runny surface of the omelette before folding, reserving a little to scatter over the finished omelette. Crisped bacon can be crumbled in with the cheese. If the cheese is very salty, use less salt when seasoning the eggs.

Cheeses that melt well, such as Durrus, Gruyère or Fontina, make excellent fillings. Lay thin slices on the omelette and flash under a hot grill before folding.

Ham fillings. Chop a slice of cooked ham with a little parsley, add a few capers if you like, and season with black pepper. Cooked asparagus tips, heated in a little butter or cream, can be added to ham or used alone.

Sorrel filling. Put a handful of young sorrel leaves, well washed and roughly chopped, in a small pan with a large lump of butter and a pinch of salt. Simmer for a few minutes and the sorrel will literally melt on the pan. Drain well and add to the omelette before folding.

LAYERED OMELETTE WITH CLONAKILTY BLACK PUDDING
SERVES 2

Black pudding as an omelette filling is said to be an invention from Normandy, using, of course, French *boudin* or *andouillette*. Nearer home, the excellent pudding from Clonakilty, Co. Cork, is, in fact, the perfect partner for the creamy buttery eggs, with just the right degree of spiciness and texture.

For the filling, simply slice or cube 75–100 g/3–4 oz/¾ cup of black pudding and sauté in a little butter or oil until it is beginning to crisp.

To make a layered omelette for 2 people, make the first omelette as described on page 38 but don't fold it. Simply slide onto a warmed plate, runny side up. Spread the filling evenly over the top. Quickly make the next omelette, slide it onto a warm buttered plate and invert over the filling. Divide the omelette in half and serve immediately on warm plates.

For more people simply add more layers, varying the fillings if you prefer. Leave the runny sides uppermost until the final layer. If the omelettes need to be reheated lay a few shavings of butter over the top and reheat briefly in a gentle oven. Cut into wedges, like a cake. Four layers will serve 4 people.

TORTILLA

SERVES 4 WITH A SALAD FOR LUNCH

One of Spain's most popular dishes, the tortilla is eaten at any time of day or night. It can be cut into tiny slices for tapas and served with drinks, and no Spanish picnic takes place without a tortilla. The following is the basic recipe. There are more elaborate versions with ham or chorizo, peppers, courgettes, aubergines and sometimes fish, but the method is the same.

For the quantities given below, a 20 cm/8 inch pan is about the right size. The finished tortilla should be about 2.5–3.5 cm/1–1.5 inches deep. For this style of omelette slow cooking over low heat is needed.

- ■ 450 g/1 lb/1¼ cups potatoes
- ■ 1 medium onion
- ■ olive oil
- ■ 6 large eggs
- ■ 1 tablespoon parsley, finely chopped
- ■ salt and black pepper

Peel the potatoes and cut into small cubes. Peel the onion and slice finely. Heat the pan and when just hot enough to sizzle put in 3 tablespoons of olive oil. When the oil is hot add the onions and potatoes. Cook over a moderate heat without browning, stirring from time to time, until the onions are transparent and the potatoes are starting to soften.

Beat the eggs gently together and season well. Lower the heat. Pour the eggs over the potato mixture, stirring here and there to allow the eggs to reach the bottom. Continue to cook very slowly, shaking the pan from time to time and sliding a spatula around the edges and underneath to prevent burning. When the eggs are set but the top is still a little liquid, invert the tortilla onto a warm plate, add a little oil to the pan and slide the uncooked side back into the pan to finish cooking. If you prefer, the top can be finished under a hot grill. Turn out onto a warm plate and allow to cool a little — it is usually served warm or at room temperature. Sprinkle the parsley on top.

TOMATO AND CHEESE FRITTATA
SERVES 4

Italy's famous omelette is the frittata and unlike the French omelette the eggs are well beaten before adding the filling, which gives the characteristic thin flat shape.

- 6 eggs
- 100 g/4 oz/²⁄₃ cup grated Parmesan and Gruyère or sliced goat's cheese
- 2 tablespoons basil
- 4 ripe tomatoes, peeled, seeded and chopped or 2 soft sundried tomatoes
- 15 g/½ oz/1 tablespoon butter
- 1 tablespoon olive oil
- salt and freshly ground black pepper

Crack the eggs into a bowl. Add the seasoning and beat the eggs together thoroughly. Reserve 2 tablespoons of the cheese, stir in the remainder, the torn basil leaves and the tomatoes and mix well. Heat a 25 cm/10 inch pan over a moderate heat, add the oil and butter and when the butter has stopped foaming, pour in the egg mixture. Lower the heat and cook gently until the eggs have set and just a little runny egg remains on top. Sprinkle the reserved cheese over the top and then slide the pan under a hot grill for a few moments to finish the cooking, but don't let it brown too much.

Allow the frittata to cool slightly before sliding it onto a serving plate. Serve it cut in wedges like a cake.

MARINATED CHICKEN WITH RED PEPPER OMELETTES
SERVES 4 TO 6

All around the shores of the southern Mediterranean there are interesting recipes combining eggs with meat, dishes with very ancient roots, reflecting the fusion of Arab, Greek and Italian cultures stretching far back into antiquity. In this recipe, adapted from Robert Carrier's magical book, *A Taste of Morocco*, chicken joints are marinated in 'chermoula', a spicy, aromatic, dry marinade extensively used in Moroccan cooking, and garnished with paper-thin omelettes. The contrast between the spicy meat and the velvety omelettes is unusually good.

■ 6–8 chicken pieces, leg joints or breasts

Note: If chicken breasts are used, add 2 tablespoons of olive oil to the chermoula to moisten the drier meat.

Chermoula

■ 1 Spanish onion
■ 4 tablespoons each parsley and coriander
■ 2 teaspoons each paprika, grated ginger and ground cumin or cumin seeds
■ ½ teaspoon each cayenne pepper and cinnamon
■ rind of 1 lemon or 1 preserved lemon
■ salt and black pepper
■ 3 tablespoons whole almonds, to garnish

Omelettes

- 8 large eggs
- 2 tablespoons flat-leafed parsley, coarsely chopped
- ½ red pepper, seeded and very finely chopped
- oil
- salt, black pepper and a pinch of ground cumin

Put all the chermoula ingredients into a food processor and pulse until finely chopped, or chop with a sharp knife. Rub this mixture thoroughly into the chicken pieces, cover with clingfilm and refrigerate for several hours or overnight.

When ready to cook, transfer the chicken to an oven dish, pouring in all the marinade juices. Cover loosely with foil and bake at 200°C/400°F/ Gas 6 for 45–50 minutes, removing the foil for the last 20 minutes to brown the chicken. If chicken breasts are used, reduce the cooking time and test after 30 minutes.

To make the omelettes, beat the eggs well for a few moments, then add the parsley, red pepper and seasonings. Heat a 20 cm/8 inch pan, add a teaspoon of oil and when it's hot pour in a small ladle of egg (about 3–4 tablespoons). Swirl the egg around the pan to spread it evenly, as though making a thin pancake, and cook until the top is just set. Slide onto a sheet of baking paper and cook the remaining egg mixture in the same manner, lowering the heat if the pan gets too hot — the omelettes should not brown too much but remain soft and pliable. This quantity will make 8–10 omelettes. The omelettes can be made while the chicken is cooking, or even earlier, and reheated for 5 minutes in the oven.

While the pan is still hot, toss the almonds until they begin to colour slightly. Drain on kitchen paper and sprinkle very lightly with salt.

To serve, arrange the chicken on a heated serving dish or individual plates and place 1 or 2 omelettes, folded in four, on top of each serving. Scatter the almonds and any remaining parsley or coriander over the top.

A rice pilaff or a salad of broad beans with grilled red peppers and tomatoes can be served on the side.

Note: Chermoula also makes an excellent marinade for a loin or leg of lamb.

ROLLED OMELETTES WITH SALMON AND LEEK FILLING AND SPICY VINAIGRETTE
SERVES 4 AS A FIRST COURSE

These rolled omelettes can be eaten either hot or cold. If eaten cold, both omelettes and filling can be made in advance and put together when you are ready to eat.

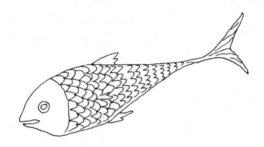

Salmon and leek filling

- ■ 15–25 g/½–1 oz/1–2 tablespoons butter
- ■ 225 g/8 oz/1½ cups cleaned leeks, finely chopped
- ■ 1 clove garlic, finely chopped
- ■ 4 scallions, finely chopped
- ■ 1 tablespoon parsley, finely chopped
- ■ 1–2 tablespoons Vermouth
- ■ 3 tablespoons crème fraîche
- ■ 2 teaspoons lemon juice
- ■ 225 g/8 oz/1 cup poached and flaked salmon
- ■ salt and cayenne pepper

Omelettes

- ■ 4 eggs
- ■ 1 tablespoon crème fraîche or cream
- ■ olive oil
- ■ salt and black pepper
- ■ Spicy Vinaigrette (page 122)
- ■ watercress or coriander, to garnish

Melt the butter in a pan, add the leeks, garlic, scallions and parsley and cook slowly until tender. Add the Vermouth, raise the heat and boil hard for a few moments. Transfer the mixture to a blender or processor, add the crème fraîche and purée until the mixture is smooth. Season well, adding lemon juice, salt and cayenne pepper to taste.

To make the omelettes, beat the eggs together with the crème fraîche and season well. Heat a 15 cm/6 inch pan until hot, add a teaspoon of oil and when it is hot add a quarter of the egg mixture, turning the pan to spread the mixture evenly, as though making a pancake. Lower the heat so the omelettes will cook gently and remain pliable. Cook until the top has just set. Slide onto baking paper and make 3 more omelettes.

When ready to serve, fold the salmon into the leek mixture, spread a quarter over each of the 4 omelettes, roll up and arrange on the plates. Spoon a little Spicy Vinaigrette over the omelettes and drizzle a little around the plates. Finally, garnish with little bunches of watercress or coriander.

OMELETTE ARNOLD BENNETT
SERVES 2

This was the favourite omelette of the novelist and critic, Arnold Bennett, created for him at the Savoy Hotel in London in the 1920s where it is still served today.

- 40 g/1½ oz/3 tablespoons butter
- 4–5 tablespoons double cream
- 150 g/5 oz/1 cup cooked and flaked smoked haddock
- 5 large eggs
- 4 tablespoons grated Parmesan
- black pepper

Melt a tablespoon of butter with a tablespoon of the cream in a small pan. Add the fish and toss gently until warm. Beat the eggs together lightly and stir in the fish mixture. Season to taste with pepper. Make the omelette in the usual way (see page 38), using a 25 cm/10 inch pan, and when it is just set underneath, but still rather runny, spread the cheese and remaining cream evenly over the top. Brown under a hot grill and serve at once.

SWEET BAKED SOUFFLÉ OMELETTE
SERVES 2–3

For this type of omelette the separated egg whites are stiffly beaten before being folded into the yolks, giving the light foamy texture of a soufflé. This quantity makes a speedy and delicious dessert for two or three — for more people it's best to make two omelettes. A 25 cm/10 inch pan or oven dish is about the right size.

- 4 large eggs
- 2 tablespoons caster sugar
- ¼ teaspoon vanilla extract
- 2–3 tablespoons good jam
- 15 g/½ oz/1 tablespoon butter for the pan

Heat the oven to 180°C/350°F/Gas 4. Gently warm the oven dish or pan and butter well.

Separate the eggs and beat the yolks well with the sugar and vanilla extract. Whip the whites until they stand in soft, glistening peaks. Beat 1 tablespoon of the whipped whites into the egg yolks to loosen them, before lightly folding the yolk mixture into the remaining whites with a large metal spoon.

Pour the mixture into the buttered dish and bake for 8–12 minutes or until the omelette is puffed and golden and just set on the top. Remove from the oven and, with a knife, draw a deep line from side to side across the centre of the omelette. Spread the jam on top and slide the omelette out onto a warm serving plate, folding it over along the line as it leaves the dish. Sprinkle a little more sugar and a few thin flakes of butter over the top and serve immediately.

4

Impeccable Scrambled Eggs

Whether for breakfast, supper or a snack in between, almost everyone loves scrambled eggs. They are often cooked in a hurry, however, and consequently end up rather dry and lumpy. Taking a little more time and being a little more generous with the butter can, on the other hand, transform a simple snack into a sublime dish of delicate creamy curds. The secret is gentle heat, slow constant stirring and a heavy-bottomed pan that conducts heat evenly.

The ideal proportions for 2 people are 35 g/1¼ oz/2 tablespoons of butter to 4 large eggs and the eggs should be well beaten together for even cooking. If calories are a consideration, less butter can be used or use a mixture of low fat crème fraîche and butter. The finished dish won't have quite the same unctuous texture but it will be very good.

Put one-third of the butter into a saucepan and allow it to melt gently. Cut the remaining butter into small cubes and add half to the 4 beaten eggs. As soon as the butter in the pan has melted pour in the eggs and begin to stir firmly, using a wooden spoon or spatula, and scraping the bottom and sides of the pan as you go. The eggs will gradually begin to thicken. The moment they approach the consistency you are aiming for, take the pan off the heat — they will continue to cook in their own heat. When the eggs are just as you like them, stir in the remaining cold butter, which stops the cooking and adds to the creaminess. Serve immediately with hot buttered toast.

Delicious as they are unadorned, you may want to add some interesting flavours such as asparagus tips, grated courgettes or other light vegetables. These should be softened first in a little butter (use the microwave) and added to the eggs just before they thicken. Add uncooked flavourings such as grated cheese, ham, crisped bacon, smoked salmon, etc. at this point, too.

HOT BUTTERED ROLLS WITH SCRAMBLED EGGS AND SMOKED SALMON
SERVES 4

A variation on hot buttered toast, bread rolls are hollowed out, crisped in the oven and filled with the eggs and salmon. Fresh Tomato Sauce (page 122) can be served on the side.

- 4 crusty round rolls, about 10 cm/4 inches wide
- 40 g/1½ oz/3 tablespoons butter for rolls or olive oil
- 8 large eggs
- 65 g/2½ oz/5 tablespoons butter for eggs
- 4 medium slices smoked salmon
- 2 teaspoons capers
- 4 slices of lemon
- 1 tablespoon finely chopped dill or parsley
- salt and black pepper

Cut the rolls in half horizontally, remove some of the crumb and brush the insides with the softened butter. Crisp the rolls in a hot oven at 200°C/400°F/Gas 6 for about 5 minutes, keeping an eye on them as they can burn in a flash.

Make the scrambled eggs as described on page 53. Season to taste.

Pile the eggs into 4 of the shell halves, letting any surplus egg spill over onto the plate. Fold or pleat the slices of smoked salmon into the remaining shells. Garnish the salmon with the capers and a slice of lemon. Spoon a little pool of the warmed sauce onto each plate, lightly dust the eggs and salmon with the chopped dill and serve immediately.

PIPERADE

SERVES 4 FOR LUNCH OR A LIGHT SUPPER

There are many dishes from the south of France and northern Spain in which vegetables, sausages, ham or cheese are first cooked together to form a sort of stew before beaten eggs are added and very gently scrambled. The Piperade from the Basque country is probably the best known of these and it is said to have been popularised by Marcel Boulestin, whose rather vague but quite inspirational cookery books introduced English-speaking readers to wonderful 'foreign' food in the 1920s and 30s.

- 2–3 tablespoons oil
- 1 medium onion, finely chopped
- 1–2 cloves garlic, finely chopped
- 3 large red or green peppers, seeded and cut into 1 cm/½ inch strips
- 6 large tomatoes, skinned, seeded and chopped
- thyme and basil, to taste
- 6 large eggs
- 4 thick slices cooked ham or bacon, to garnish (optional)
- salt and black pepper

Heat the oil in a large pan and add the onion and garlic. Cook until the onion begins to soften, then add the peppers and finally the chopped tomatoes. Season well, add the thyme and basil and cook until the peppers have softened and the tomatoes are almost melting.

Pour in the beaten eggs, lower the heat and stir gently until they just begin to thicken. Take the pan off the heat and allow the Piperade to stand for a few minutes while the eggs finish cooking. Pour the contents of the pan into a heated serving dish or onto individual plates. Garnish with the ham, previously heated in the oven or under the grill, and serve with good bread, a salad and red wine.

VOL-AU-VENTS WITH SCRAMBLED EGGS AND SHRIMPS
SERVES 4

Bought frozen vol-au-vent cases make ideal containers for this easy-to-prepare starter or lunch dish. Dress them up with Red Pepper Sauce (page 127). Alternative ideas for cases are given below.

- 4 king-size vol-au-vent cases
- 5–6 large eggs
- 50 g/2 oz/4 tablespoons butter
- 100–150 g/4–5 oz/¾ cup cooked shrimps or prawns
- 1 tablespoon chopped chives or chervil
- 2 tablespoons vinaigrette
- salt and cayenne pepper
- salad leaves, to garnish

Bake the vol-au-vents as directed on the packet and keep warm. Make the scrambled eggs as described on page 53. As the eggs begin to thicken, add the shrimps previously warmed in a little hot water and drained well. Finally add the herbs and seasonings. Divide the mixture between the pastry cases. Garnish with the lightly dressed salad leaves and spoon a little of the Red Pepper Sauce attractively on the plates.

Alternative Cases

Bread tartlets

Cut circles about 7.5 cm/3 inches in diameter from slices of fresh white bread, dip in melted butter and press into small tartlet tins. Bake at 180°C/350°F/Gas 4 for 12–15 minutes until nicely coloured. Cool on a wire rack. Fill with scrambled eggs or finely chopped hard-boiled eggs bound with mayonnaise and flavoured with chives.

Potato nests

Put 750 g/1½ lb peeled boiled potatoes through a ricer or mash until smooth. Work in 25 g/1 oz/2 tablespoons of butter, 2 egg yolks and seasoning and beat until smooth and creamy. Add a tablespoon of cream if necessary. Pipe rings onto baking paper, starting in the centre and working outwards to about 7.5 cm/3 inches in diameter, then pipe one ring on top of the outer ring to form a wall. Brush with beaten egg and brown in a hot oven at 220°C/425°F/Gas 7 for 8–10 minutes. Fill with scrambled eggs or poached eggs topped with Sauce Mornay (page 121).

Stuffed tomatoes

Cut lids from the tops of large beef tomatoes and scoop out the contents with a spoon, reserving them for soup. Put the tomatoes upside down in a warm oven for 5–6 minutes until just warmed through. Fill with scrambled eggs, garnish with crisp bacon and serve on toast or fried bread.

SWISS-STYLE EGGS
SERVES 4

Use any good melting cheese such as Durrus, Gruyère or Emmenthal for this interesting scrambled egg variation.

- 50 g/2 oz/4 tablespoons butter
- ½ medium red onion, finely chopped
- 150 ml/¼ pint/⅝ cup white wine
- 175 g/6 oz/1 cup grated cheese
- 1 large tablespoon chopped chervil or parsley
- 7 large eggs
- 3 slices white bread, cut into fingers and fried
- black pepper and mace or nutmeg

Melt the butter in a deep sauté pan, add the onion and cook until softened. Lower the heat and pour in the wine, stirring well. Add the cheese, chervil and seasoning and simmer gently, stirring well until the cheese has melted.

Separate the eggs and beat the whites to stiff, glistening peaks. Beat the yolks together thoroughly, work in a tablespoon of the whites to loosen the mixture, then fold the yolks lightly into the whites. Pour the egg mixture into the pan, blending it well into the cheese sauce. Continue stirring until a soft, lightly scrambled mass is formed. Transfer to a heated serving dish and surround with the fingers of fried bread. Serve immediately.

COLD SCRAMBLED EGGS WITH MAYONNAISE
SERVES 4

This unexpectedly good cold starter is adapted from Margaret Costa's *Four Seasons* cookery book.

- 6 large eggs
- 50 g/2 oz/4 tablespoons butter
- 100–175 g/4–6 oz/½–¾ cup chopped smoked salmon, smoked trout or cooked salmon
- 2 tablespoons cream
- 2 tablespoons chopped chives and dill or parsley
- 150 ml/¼ pint/⅝ cup mayonnaise (page 123) or Sauce Remoulade (page 126)
- milk, for thinning
- rocket or salad leaves, to garnish
- 2–3 tablespoons vinaigrette for salad dressing
- salt and black pepper

Scramble the eggs in the butter as described on page 53. As soon as the eggs begin to thicken, gently mix in the fish, cream and 1 tablespoon of herbs. Season well, being cautious with salt if the salmon is on the salty side.

Pile the eggs in a little dome on a serving dish and when they are quite cold, thin the mayonnaise or Remoulade with a little milk to the texture of thick cream and pour over the eggs.

Scatter the remaining herbs on top and surround with the dressed salad leaves.

SCRAMBLED EGGS WITH SAUTÉED KIDNEYS
SERVES 4 FOR BREAKFAST, LUNCH OR SUPPER

'The kidney is loved by the mushroom scarce less tenderly than the egg.' Elizabeth Pennell, *Feasts of Autolycus*

For the kidneys

- 8 lamb's kidneys
- 25 g/1 oz/2 tablespoons butter
- 1 tablespoon cream
- salt and cayenne pepper

For the eggs

- 25 g/1oz/2 tablespoons butter
- 12 small mushrooms, sliced
- 6 large eggs
- 3 tablespoons cream
- salt and black pepper
- 12 triangles of buttered toast
- 1 tablespoon chopped chives

Peel the fine membrane from the kidneys and cut them in half. Using a pair of scissors, snip out the white core and discard. Slice the kidneys thinly. Melt the butter in a medium sauté pan and when it's hot, but before it browns, put in the cream and the kidneys, stirring them about for 3–4 minutes until they are cooked but still slightly pink. Season them with salt and enough cayenne pepper to make them nicely spicy. Keep warm while preparing the eggs and toast.

Put the second amount of butter in a small saucepan and sauté the mushrooms. When they are tender, push them to one side and pour in the beaten eggs and cream, stirring gently until the eggs are somewhat thickened and the mixture creamy. Season well, adding plenty of black pepper.

Pour the kidneys onto a heated serving plate, make a well in the centre to hold the eggs and arrange the triangles of toast around the dish. Sprinkle with the chives and serve hot.

5

Quiches, Tarts and Baked Egg Dishes

ARDRAHAN CHEESE TART
SERVES 6 AS A FIRST COURSE

Ardrahan cheese lends its distinctive flavour to this lovely tart. It is at its best hot but very good cold, too. Any good melting cheese such as Gruyère, Emmenthal or Durrus can be used as well.

- 225 g/8 oz homemade or frozen puff pastry
- 225 g/8 oz/1 cup ripe Ardrahan cheese
- 150 ml/¼ pint/⅝ cup cream
- 4 beaten egg yolks
- salt, black pepper and cayenne pepper
- nutmeg
- salad leaves, to garnish

Heat the oven to 180°C/350°F/Gas 4. Line a round tart tin with the pastry.

Remove any hard pieces of crust from the cheese and cut into cubes. Mix the cubes with half the cream and put into a small bowl over hot water. Allow the cheese to melt very slowly, stirring until smooth, then add it to the beaten eggs. Pour in the rest of the cream, mixing together thoroughly. Season with black pepper, nutmeg, a pinch of cayenne pepper and add salt to taste.

Pour the mixture into the prepared pastry case and bake for 10 minutes. Lower the heat to 170°C/325°F/Gas 3 and bake for a further 30 minutes until the pastry is cooked and the filling puffed and golden brown. The tart, which will deflate rather quickly, can be served immediately or allow to cool. Garnish with salad leaves.

BACON QUICHE WITH PEAS
SERVES 6 AS A FIRST COURSE OR
4 FOR LUNCH

Possibly the best quiche of all, and certainly the best known, is the Quiche Lorraine. There are many interpretations of this famous tart and in this case the addition of tiny peas (petits pois) offers an interesting contrast in flavour and colour to the smoked bacon of the traditional recipe.

- shortcrust pastry to line a 25 cm/10 inch tart tin
- 175 g/6 oz/1⅓ cups fresh or frozen petits pois
- 150 g/5 oz/1 cup smoked bacon or bacon rashers, cubed
- 1 teaspoon oil
- 3 large eggs
- 2 egg yolks
- 300 ml/½ pint/1¼ cups cream

- 50 g/2 oz/½ cup Gruyère or strong Cheddar cheese, grated
- salt and black pepper

Line the spring form tart tin with the pastry and leave to rest in the fridge while preparing the filling. Put a baking sheet in the oven and set the oven at 200°C/400°F/Gas 6.

Put the peas in a strainer and pour boiling water over them to defrost. If using fresh peas, cook until just tender. Heat a small pan and cook the bacon slowly in the oil until crisp. Drain on kitchen paper. Beat the eggs, yolks and cream together lightly, season well and add half the grated cheese. Spread the bacon over the pastry base, cover with the well-drained peas and gently pour in the cream and egg mixture. Sprinkle the remaining cheese over the top and slide the tin onto the baking sheet.

Bake for 10 minutes, then lower the heat to 160°C/325°F/Gas 3 for a further 30 minutes or until the pastry is cooked and the filling set but very slightly wobbly when the tin is shaken gently.

Allow to rest for 15 minutes before serving.

Note: To make an excellent Crab Quiche, replace the peas with 225 g/8 oz of white crab meat, the cheese with Parmesan and reduce the bacon to 50g/2 oz. Sharpen the flavour with the grated rind of half a lemon and follow the directions above.

BROCCOLI AND PINE NUT TART
SERVES 6 AS A STARTER

- 1 tablespoon sultanas
- shortcrust pastry to line a 25 cm/10 inch spring form tart tin
- 225 g/8 oz/2 cups broccoli florets
- 1 teaspoon cumin seeds
- 50 g/2 oz/⅓ cup pine nuts
- 4 large eggs plus 1 egg yolk
- 300 ml/½ pint/1¼ cups cream
- nutmeg, to taste
- salt and black pepper

Set the oven at 200°C/400°F/Gas 6. Put the sultanas in a small dish with a little hot water to plump up for a few minutes.

Put a baking sheet into the oven to heat. Line the tart tin with the pastry.

Blanch the broccoli florets in boiling salted water for 4 minutes until they are just beginning to soften, then immediately immerse in cold water to chill. When cool, drain the broccoli and squeeze gently in a tea towel to remove as much moisture as possible before arranging on the pastry.

Heat a small pan and briefly toast the cumin seeds and pine nuts, watching carefully as they burn easily. Add these to the broccoli with the drained sultanas.

Beat the eggs, the extra yolk and the cream together, season generously, adding a pinch of nutmeg, and pour over the broccoli. Put the tart on the baking sheet, lowering the heat after 10 minutes to 160°C/325°F/Gas 3. Cook for a further 35–45 minutes until the pastry is cooked and the tart is set with just a slight wobble when the tin is gently shaken. Cool slightly before serving.

EASTER PIE

SERVES 10 AS A SUBSTANTIAL FIRST COURSE OR 6 AS A MAIN COURSE

This rich pie from Italy, traditional in the Piedmont area at Easter, combines spinach and artichokes with ricotta cheese and eggs, and as artichokes are often hard to find even in season, tins or jars will do very well. Ricotta is widely available, but at a pinch cottage cheese can be used.

- 450 g/1 lb/9 cups fresh spinach
- 100 ml/4 fl oz/½ cup/4 tablespoons olive oil
- 1 x 350 g/12 oz jar artichoke hearts or bottoms
- 2 tablespoons chopped fresh or 1 teaspoon dried oregano
- 350 g/12 oz/2 cups ricotta
- juice of ½ lemon
- 2–3 cloves of garlic, very finely chopped
- 50 g/2 oz/ ⅓ cup each Parmesan and Cheddar, grated
- 9 large eggs
- 1 packet frozen puff pastry
- salt and black pepper

Set the oven to 180°C/350°F/Gas 4. You will need a spring form tin approx. 23–25 cm/9–10 inches.

Wash the spinach well in salted water and remove any thick stalks. Heat 2 tablespoons of oil in a large pan. Shake the spinach dry and add to the pan, tossing about until it has just wilted and released its moisture. It will probably be necessary to cook the spinach in two lots. Squeeze dry and chop roughly.

Rinse the artichokes in warm water and drain well. Chop roughly and put in a large bowl with the spinach, oregano, ricotta, lemon juice, garlic, cheese and 2 beaten eggs. Mix well together and season generously.

Roll out the pastry thinly, allowing two-thirds to line the tin and the remainder to make the lid. Butter a 23–25 cm/9–10 inch spring form tin generously and line with pastry, allowing a small overlap at the top. Pack the filling into the tin. With the back of a spoon and spacing them in a circle, make six deep depressions in the filling. Slide an egg into each of these, cracking them first into a saucer to avoid any broken yolks.

Cover with the pastry lid, moistening the edges lightly with water. Press the pastry sides and top together, pinching with the fingers to make a decorative edge. Trim off any surplus pastry and use to make leaves. Make 2 or 3 small steam holes in the lid. Beat the remaining egg and brush generously over the top of the pie.

Bake for about 1 hour until the pastry is puffed and golden brown. Lower the heat slightly and cover the top with foil if it appears to be browning too quickly. Allow it to cool for 15–20 minutes before serving, then cut into wedges like a cake. The pie can also be served cold and, in fact, the flavour improves if kept for a day or two. It is an ideal pie for picnics and parties, too.

MALTESE BEEF AND EGG PIE
SERVES 8 AS A MAIN COURSE

The cuisine of Malta has an affinity with that of Sicily and this pie is a homely reflection of that magnificent confection so eloquently described in Giuseppe Lampedusa's moving novel of Sicilian life, *The Leopard*. Chicken livers are not always easy to find and if they are not available, increase the quantity of beef. They do, however, give a subtle flavour and texture to the sauce and it is worthwhile trying to find them.

- 350 g/12 oz/6 cups fresh spinach
- 2 tablespoons olive oil
- 1 large Spanish onion, finely chopped
- 1 carrot, grated
- 100 g/4 oz/¾ cup mushrooms
- 550 g/1¼ lb/2½ cups minced beef
- 2 bacon rashers, chopped
- 100 g/4 oz/¾ cup chicken livers
- 1 tablespoon tomato purée
- ¼ teaspoon mace or nutmeg

- a pinch of cinnamon
- 4 large eggs
- 1 packet frozen puff pastry
- 4 hard-boiled eggs
- 1 beaten egg
- salt and black pepper

Wash the spinach in salted water, remove any hard stems and drain. Heat a large frying pan with 1 tablespoon of oil and put in the spinach, stirring until it is just wilted. Squeeze out the moisture and set aside.

In a large saucepan sauté the onion, carrot and mushrooms until soft. In a separate pan brown the meat and the bacon. Add to the mushroom mixture. Put the chopped livers into the empty pan, add a spoonful of oil and toss until the livers are lightly browned but still pink inside. Add these to the meat and vegetables. Stir in the tomato purée, seasoning and spices. Cover the saucepan and simmer very gently for 15–20 minutes. Allow the mixture to cool before beating in the 4 whole eggs. Check the seasoning.

Roll out the pastry thinly and use two-thirds to line a 25 cm/10 inch spring form tin or oven dish, keeping the remainder to form a lid.

Spoon the meat and vegetable mixture into the tin and level the top. Arrange the sliced hard-boiled eggs in a layer and finally cover with the spinach.

Put on the pastry lid, dampening the edges and pinching together decoratively. Make 1 or 2 slits in the lid, brush with beaten egg and bake for 45 minutes at 190°C/375°F/ Gas 5. Remove from the oven and allow the pie to cool for 15–20 minutes before removing from the tin. Cut into wedges for serving. The pie is also very good cold and keeps very well for 2–3 days.

LAMB KOFTAS WITH EGGS
SERVES 6

This dish of spicy lamb meatballs is from the rich Moroccan repertoire of recipes combining eggs with meat. Although the list of ingredients is long, they are readily available and both koftas and sauce are quick to prepare.

- 750 g/1¾ lb/3½ cups lean minced lamb
- 1 large Spanish onion
- 50 g/2 oz/1 cup breadcrumbs
- 1–2 tablespoons olive oil
- ½ teaspoon each cumin, cayenne pepper, cinnamon, paprika and ginger
- 15 g/½ oz/1 tablespoon butter
- 6 eggs
- salt and black pepper

Sauce

- 550 g/1¼ lb tomatoes, skinned, seeded and chopped *or* 400 ml/15 fl oz/2 cups tinned chopped Italian tomatoes
- 1 Spanish onion, finely chopped
- 4 tablespoons each chopped coriander and parsley
- 2–3 cloves garlic
- 2 tablespoons olive oil
- 2 teaspoons paprika
- ½ teaspoon each cayenne pepper and cumin
- 1 large piece of ginger, grated
- 150 ml/¼ pint/⅝ cup water
- salt and black pepper

For the sauce, put all the ingredients into a medium saucepan and simmer gently for about 35 minutes. Set aside.

Heat the oven to 190°C/375°F/Gas 5.

To make the koftas, put the lamb, roughly chopped onion, spices, breadcrumbs, olive oil and seasonings into a food processor and work until the mixture is fairly smooth, but don't let it become a paste. Taste for seasoning. It should be very spicy and slightly hot.

Take heaped teaspoonfuls of the mixture and shape into small balls about 25 cm/1 inch in diameter, using your hands. Sauté these gently in butter until lightly browned — they will need to be done in 2 batches. Transfer the koftas to an oven dish, pour the prepared sauce over them and bake for 15 minutes. Lower the heat to 150°C/300°F/Gas 2.

Beat the eggs together lightly and season well. Remove the dish from the oven and pour the eggs over the top. Cover the dish with foil and bake for a further 8–10 minutes until the eggs are just set, taking care not to overcook them as part of the charm of this dish lies in the soft and tender texture of the eggs.

BAKED EGGS WITH BACON AND OYSTERS
SERVES 4

- 12 oysters
- 15 g/½ oz/1 tablespoon butter
- 4–5 medium slices smoked streaky bacon, chopped
- 175 g/6 oz/1¾ cups sliced mushrooms
- 8 large eggs
- 175 ml/6 fl oz/¾ cup double cream
- Tabasco or cayenne pepper
- salt and black pepper

Butter 4 small oven dishes that will each hold 2 eggs or use 1 large dish. Open the oysters and reserve their liquid.

Melt the butter in a small pan and cook the bacon until lightly crisped. Drain and divide between the 4 dishes. Add the mushrooms to the same pan and cook until they are just beginning to brown slightly. Add to the bacon, moisten with a little oyster liquid and season with black pepper.

Put 3 oysters into each dish and with the back of a spoon make 2 small depressions to hold the eggs. Slide an egg into each depression, pour the cream over them and season with 1 drop of Tabasco or a pinch of cayenne pepper. Salt will probably not be necessary.

Bake for about 10 minutes at 180°C/350°F/Gas 4 until the whites are set but the yolks still soft.

EGGS BAKED WITH SPINACH
SERVES 4

For these eggs you will need 4 of the little round oven-proof dishes called cocottes or ramekins. The spinach can be replaced with sliced mushrooms cooked in a little butter for a change.

- 225 g/8 oz/4 cups spinach
- 3 streaky bacon rashers
- 15 g/1 oz/1 tablespoon butter
- soy sauce
- 4 large eggs
- 150 ml/¼ pint/⅝ cup cream
- 2 tablespoons chopped chervil or chives
- salt and black pepper

Preheat the oven to 180°C/350°F/Gas 4. Remove the stalks from the spinach and wash carefully. Chop roughly, place in a small pan with half the butter and cook gently until just tender. Squeeze out as much moisture as possible. Chop the bacon and cook in the remaining butter until crisp.

Butter 4 ramekins. Put a tablespoon of spinach in each, scatter a little bacon on top and season well, adding 2–3 drops of soy sauce to each dish. Crack the eggs, one at a time, into a saucer and slide on top of the bacon. Divide the cream between the dishes and sprinkle the herbs over the top. Set the ramekins in a baking tin and add warm water to come two-thirds up the sides. Cover loosely with foil and bake for about 15 minutes until the whites are set and the yolks still soft. Delicious served with Melba toast or brown bread.

To make Melba toast, toast a slice of fresh white sliced pan on each side under a hot grill. With a sharp knife and working quickly before the bread cools, cut off the crusts, place the bread flat on a board and split in two horizontally, giving two slices of very thin bread. Brown the un-toasted sides briefly under the grill. Make plenty as there is rarely any left. It can be made a few hours ahead of time.

6
Soufflés

Making a Soufflé

The soufflé has an undeserved reputation as a rather tricky and temperamental creation, though in fact its success is more or less assured and the only tricky aspects are how far to beat the egg whites and when to take the soufflé from the oven. Once mastered with a trial run in your own oven, there are few dishes that taste as good, need no special ingredients and give such a dramatic effect for so little cost. Soufflés can even be prepared in advance and frozen, ready to cook when the occasion demands.

To get the maximum volume from the egg whites, the choice of bowl used for beating them needs a little thought. Top of the list is an unlined copper bowl made especially for the purpose, but stainless steel, porcelain or pyrex are perfectly adequate. Don't use a plastic bowl, no matter how thoroughly it's washed, as by its nature it retains fat and the smallest trace of fat will prevent the whites reaching their full volume — the same reason why no wisp of yolk must get into the whites before they are beaten. The eggs should be at room temperature for best results.

For soufflés and mousses the egg whites should be beaten until they stand in soft peaks when the beater is lifted — peaks that fall over very slightly at the tip and are still shiny and glistening. When overbeaten they begin to look dry and break into lumps. Once this stage is reached they can't be folded into the base mixture without losing most of the precious air. It's not a bad idea for the complete novice to beat up a couple of egg whites for experimental purposes, carefully observing the different stages. Otherwise it's difficult to know just what to look for from written descriptions.

As soon as the soufflé is ready it should be served, though it can wait for 5 minutes or so in the turned-off oven. Soufflés are best made for small numbers, who are happy to sit at the table with a glass of wine and wait for the soufflé, not the other way around.

The best soufflé dishes are made from white oven china which allows the heat to penetrate quickly, but a cake tin or an oven dish with straight sides will do. Thick heavy dishes will take slightly longer to cook. Individual small dishes (ramekins) can also be used with the cooking time shortened correspondingly. Dishes should be well buttered to allow the mixture to slide up the sides while cooking.

Most recipes serve 4. If there are more people, it's easier to make 2 soufflés.

Put the soufflé in the middle of the oven, removing the upper rack as it can rise through this. The soufflé will take between 20–35 minutes to cook and it is best not to open the oven door to check for at least 18 minutes. At this point open it just enough to give the dish a little shake. If the soufflé looks as though it could topple over, cook for a further 5 minutes until it is golden brown and puffed high above the dish. The inside should be a little runny, another reason for serving it immediately as it will continue to cook in its own heat and that very important juicy centre will be lost.

For extra interest and flavour, sauces are sometimes served with soufflés. They also help to compensate for any slight overcooking!

BASIC CHEESE SOUFFLÉ
SERVES 4

- 200 ml/8 fl oz/1 cup milk
- 40 g/1½ oz/3 tablespoons butter
- 25 g/1 oz/2 tablespoons flour
- 4 egg yolks
- 40 g/1½ oz/4 tablespoons each Gruyère and Parmesan, grated
- 5 egg whites
- 1 extra tablespoon Parmesan, grated
- 2 tablespoons browned breadcrumbs
- salt, cayenne pepper and paprika

Heat the oven to 190°C/375°F/Gas 5 and butter a 15 cm/ 6 inch soufflé dish.

Heat the milk. Melt the butter in a small saucepan and mix in the flour, stirring for 2–3 minutes to cook the flour. Take it off the heat and gradually work in the milk, beating well with a whisk to avoid lumps. When the sauce is smooth, cook for 3–4 minutes, stirring continually, then remove from the heat and allow it to cool slightly. Beat in the egg yolks, one at a time. Add the salt, cayenne pepper and paprika to taste and finally beat in the cheese.

Whip the egg whites until they stand in soft, glistening peaks. Stir 1 tablespoon into the base mixture to loosen it, then, quickly and lightly, fold in the remainder with a large metal spoon. Spoon the mixture into the soufflé dish and spread evenly.

Make a groove with your thumb or the handle of a wooden spoon around the top of the soufflé just inside the rim of the dish to help it rise evenly. Sprinkle with the tablespoon of Parmesan and the breadcrumbs. Bake in the middle of the oven for 25–30 minutes. Dust a little paprika over the top and serve immediately from the dish.

SOUFFLÉ SURPRISE
SERVES 4

The 'surprise' is the discovery of poached eggs, still soft, when the soufflé is opened. This is something of a party piece, so it's probably wise to have a practice run for timing purposes before presenting it with a flourish.

Use the Basic Cheese Soufflé recipe above but choose a 20 cm/8 inch dish. If you only have the smaller dish, cut a strip of baking parchment 15 cm/6 inches deep and long enough to wrap around the dish. Fold the paper in two lengthways, butter one side generously, wrap around the dish, buttered side inwards, hold in place with a clothes peg or Sellotape while you tie it around with string, allowing the collar to extend 5 cm/2 inches above the rim of the dish. This is easier to do than it sounds and gives a dramatic effect when the soufflé is cooked and the paper peeled off.

- 4 eggs
- 1 cheese soufflé mixture (page 78)
- 225 g/8 oz/2 cups mushrooms, sliced and sautéed in a little butter
- salt and pepper

First poach the eggs as directed on page 22. Next make the cheese soufflé mixture and put half of it into the buttered dish. With the back of a dessert spoon, make 4 evenly spaced depressions, put a quarter of the sautéed mushrooms in each and top with a poached egg. Season well and spoon the remaining soufflé mixture over the eggs. Bake at 190°C/375°F/Gas 5 for about 30 minutes, checking as described on page 78 after 20 minutes.

SMOKED SALMON ROULADE
SERVES 6 AS A FIRST COURSE

An easily prepared roulade, served either warm or cold. The filling can be adapted to taste and to season.

- 225 g/8 oz smoked salmon or cooked smoked haddock
- 4 tablespoons double cream
- 4 eggs
- 2 tablespoons fine breadcrumbs
- 1 tablespoon grated Parmesan or Cheddar

Filling

- 1 x 225 g/8 oz/1½ cups carton ricotta cheese
- 2 teaspoons grated lemon rind
- 1 pickled gherkin, finely chopped
- 3 hard-boiled eggs, finely chopped
- 1 tablespoon grated cheese
- 2 tablespoons mixed fresh herbs such as dill, chervil and parsley
- paprika or cayenne pepper
- salt and black pepper

Line a standard size swiss roll tin (approx 25 x 35 cm/10 x 15 inches) with buttered baking parchment and cut a second sheet of parchment the same size.

To make the filling, mix together the ricotta, lemon rind, gherkin, hard-boiled eggs, grated cheese, seasoning and herbs.

To make the roulade, purée the fish in a blender or processor with the cream. Separate the eggs and work the yolks into the fish mixture. Season well and add the breadcrumbs.

Whip the egg whites to stiff, glistening peaks, loosen the fish mixture with 2 tablespoons of the beaten whites and lightly fold in the remainder. Turn into the tin and spread as evenly as possible.

Bake in the oven at 200°C/400°F/Gas 6 for 10–12 minutes. Lay the second sheet of parchment over a tea towel. The tea towel should be wrung out in hot water (which keeps the roulade warm and helps to prevent it cracking when it is rolled up again). Turn out the roulade on top and peel off the paper. Quickly trim the long sides of the roulade with a sharp knife (this helps to roll it more easily). Spread the filling and roll up from the short end. Sprinkle the remaining cheese on top and serve.

If the roulade needs to be reheated, brush the top with melted butter, scatter with a little cheese and heat in a moderate oven (150°C/300°F/Gas 2) for 5–6 minutes.

TWICE BAKED SOUFFLÉS

SERVES 4

These little soufflés are poached in a bain marie, rather like baked eggs. Their appearance is less spectacular than the usual soufflé, but the great advantage is they can be made in advance with the second baking done at the last minute. Have ready 4 buttered ramekins or similar small dishes.

- 200 ml/8 fl oz/1 cup milk
- 40 g/1½ oz/3 tablespoons butter
- 40 g/1½ oz/3 tablespoons flour
- 4 large eggs, separated
- 50 g/2 oz/¼ cup grated Parmesan
- 50 g/2 oz/¼ cup grated Emmenthal or Gruyère
- 300 ml/½ pint/1¼ cups cream
- nutmeg, cayenne pepper and paprika
- salt and black pepper

Set the oven to 180°C/350°F/Gas 4.

Heat the milk. Melt the butter in a small saucepan, work in the flour and cook, stirring well, for about 3 minutes. Take off the heat and slowly add the milk, whisking well to avoid lumps. Return to the heat, lower it slightly and continue to cook, stirring from time to time, for about 5 minutes until very thick. Allow the mixture to cool a little, then beat in the egg yolks one by one. Season generously, adding cayenne pepper to taste and a pinch of nutmeg. Beat in half the cheese.

Whip the egg whites to soft, glistening peaks and beat 1 tablespoon into the sauce to loosen it. With a large metal spoon, fold the sauce into the egg whites, cutting and folding as lightly as possible. Spoon the mixture into the buttered ramekins and place these in a baking tray or oven dish. Pour in enough warm water to come halfway up the sides of the dishes.

Bake in the centre of the oven for about 15–20 minutes until the soufflés are set and feel slightly springy when pressed. Remove to a wire rack to cool. The cooled and covered soufflés can be stored in the fridge for a few hours or overnight.

To complete the cooking, butter an oven dish that will just hold the soufflés, spread half the remaining cheese over the bottom, turn the soufflés out of the ramekins and arrange on top of the cheese. Pour the cream over them and scatter the reserved cheese over the top. Bake at 180°C/350°F/Gas 4 for 20–25 minutes until slightly puffed and golden. Dust with the paprika and serve immediately.

BROCCOLI AND HAM SOUFFLÉ

SERVES 6

This recipe calls for a 25 cm/10 inch soufflé dish. If your dish is smaller, a paper collar can be used (see Soufflé Surprise, page 80).

- 225 g/8 oz/1½ cups broccoli florets
- 500 ml/¾ pint/2½ cups milk
- 50 g/2 oz/4 tablespoons butter
- 50 g/2 oz/4 tablespoons flour
- 6 eggs, separated
- 100 g/4 oz/¾ cup cooked ham, very finely chopped
- 1 tablespoon grated Parmesan
- paprika
- salt and nutmeg
- black pepper and cayenne pepper

Set the oven to 180°C/350°F/Gas 4.

Cook the broccoli in the milk until just tender. Cool slightly, then purée the broccoli and milk together in a blender.

Melt the butter, work in the flour, stirring well, and cook for 2–3 minutes. Take off the heat, work in the milk and broccoli purée a little at a time, beating well to avoid lumps. Season very well and add nutmeg and cayenne pepper to taste. Stir until the sauce is thick and smooth.

Allow the sauce to cool slightly before beating in the egg yolks, ham and grated cheese. Stir until the cheese has melted.

Beat the egg whites to soft, glistening peaks. Mix 1 large tablespoon into the cheese sauce, then fold the sauce lightly into the remainder of the whites with a large metal spoon. Spoon the mixture into the soufflé dish, filling it two-thirds full. Make a groove with the handle of a wooden spoon around the top just inside the edge of the dish to help it rise evenly.

Bake in the centre of the oven for 25 minutes. Don't open the oven door for at least 18–20 minutes, then open it just barely enough to shake the dish slightly. If it wobbles dangerously, give it a further 5 minutes or so. It should be puffed and golden and a little runny in the centre. Dust the top with a little paprika and serve immediately.

GRAND MARNIER SOUFFLÉ
SERVES 4

This lovely soufflé has a special place in French cuisine.

- 2 sponge finger biscuits or macaroons
- 5 tablespoons Grand Marnier or brandy
- 200 ml/8 fl oz/1 cup milk
- 50 g/2 oz/¼ cup caster sugar
- 50 g/2 oz/4 tablespoons butter
- 70 g/2½ oz/ ½ cup good flour
- vanilla essence
- 4 large eggs, separated
- icing sugar

Butter a 15 cm/6 inch soufflé dish.

Crumble the biscuits in a small bowl, moisten with 1 table-spoon of the Grand Marnier and set aside. Heat the oven to 190°C/375°F/Gas 5.

Bring the milk to the boil with the sugar and set aside. Melt the butter in a saucepan and stir in the flour, stirring well for a few moments. Take off the heat and stir in the hot milk, beating well with a whisk to avoid lumps. Continue to cook, stirring, for 4 or 5 minutes. Allow the mixture to cool slightly. Mix in the remaining Grand Marnier and a few drops of vanilla, then beat in the egg yolks one at a time.

Beat the egg whites to soft, glistening peaks, add 1 table-spoon to the base sauce to loosen it, then fold the sauce gently into the remainder of the egg whites.

Spoon half the mixture into the soufflé dish, spread the soaked crumbs in a layer on top and cover with the remaining mixture. Level the top and make a groove with your finger or the handle of a wooden spoon around the dish just inside the edge to help it rise evenly. Put the soufflé in the centre of the oven and after 20 minutes, but not before, open the oven door just wide enough to give the dish a slight shake. If the soufflé wobbles as though it may topple over, give it another 5 minutes, by which time it should be golden brown and puffed high above the dish. Dredge the top with icing sugar and serve immediately.

ICED CRANBERRY SOUFFLÉ
SERVES 4

Iced soufflés, light and delicate with just enough gelatine to hold them together, make a perfect end to a meal. The cranberries can be fresh or frozen and give a good tart flavour and vibrant colour. The recipe can be adapted to other fruits, using the same proportions. Soft fruits, such as raspberries or strawberries, will not need to be pre-cooked. This quantity will fill a 15 cm/6 inch soufflé dish, using a paper collar (see Soufflé Surprise, page 80), or it can be piled up in an attractive china or glass serving dish.

- 4 tablespoons orange juice
- 1 sachet *or* 5 leaves gelatine
- 275 g/10 oz/1¾ cups cranberries
- 100 g/4 oz/½ cup golden caster sugar
- 300 ml/½ pint/1¼ cups cream
- 4 egg whites
- a few scented geranium leaves or lemon balm, to garnish

Put the orange juice in a small bowl, sprinkle on the gelatine and leave to become spongy (about 10 minutes). Put the cranberries in a saucepan with the sugar and 3 tablespoons of water, cover and simmer gently until the berries burst and become soft. Remove from the heat and allow to cool. Transfer the mixture to a blender and work to a purée. Leave the mixture in the blender.

Set the bowl with the gelatine over hot water and allow it to dissolve completely, stirring well and checking that there are no un-dissolved crystals. Add the gelatine to the contents of the blender and whiz for a moment to distribute the gelatine evenly before pouring the mixture into a large bowl. Whip the cream until thick, but still soft and floppy, and fold it into the fruit thoroughly.

Put the fruit mixture in the fridge to chill, checking it frequently, until it is just beginning to set around the edges. Whip the egg whites to shiny, soft peaks and fold into the fruit mixture. Pour into the prepared soufflé dish or pile up in large spoonfuls in your chosen dish. Allow it to set in the fridge for 2–3 hours and garnish with scented geranium leaves or lemon balm.

ICED HAM SOUFFLÉ
SERVES 6

Savoury chilled soufflés make great summer starters or lunch dishes. Smoked salmon, smoked trout or chicken can be used if preferred. Simply replace the red wine with white or with chicken stock and add plenty of lemon rind. A chicken soufflé can be spiced up with a little lemon grass or curry powder.

- 150 ml/¼ pint/⅝ cup red wine or chicken stock
- 1 sachet *or* 5 leaves gelatine
- 275 g/10 oz/1¾ cups cooked ham
- 300 ml/½ pint/1¼ cups cream
- 1 tablespoon creamy grain mustard
- 4 egg whites
- salt, black pepper and Tabasco or cayenne pepper
- dill sprigs, to garnish

Put the wine in a small bowl, sprinkle on the gelatine and leave to become spongy (about 10 minutes). Chop the ham as finely as possible. Put the cream in a large bowl and whip until it is thick but still soft and floppy before folding in the ham. Beat in the mustard and season very generously.

Put the bowl with the gelatine over hot water, stirring from time to time until it is completely dissolved. Allow it to cool slightly, then beat into the cream and ham mixture, making sure the gelatine is evenly distributed. Put the bowl in the fridge, checking it frequently, until the mixture is just beginning to set around the edges.

Whip the egg whites to shiny, soft peaks and fold into the ham mixture. Pour into the prepared soufflé dish or pile up in large spoonfuls in a shallow bowl. Return to the fridge to set for 2–3 hours. Garnish with dill sprigs.

7

Meringues and Other Delights

Meringues

While eggs have formed a vital part of man's diet from earliest times, the different culinary functions of yolks and whites were not really understood until comparatively recent days. Egg whites in particular were thought to be chilling to the blood and it wasn't until the Elizabethan age that their magical capacity for trapping air was realised and the era of 'snow cream' began. Of course, whipping them was something of a problem before the fork was in common use. Little bundles of birch twigs were used for the purpose and, though quite effective, it took a long time. Now that we can make meringues at the flick of a switch we don't value them as highly as perhaps we should.

When making meringue, the egg whites are beaten more stiffly than those for soufflés or mousses, beaten in fact to the famous 'stiff peak' stage. Caster sugar is folded in at this point, with the beating continued until the mixture is stiff again. For harder meringue, icing sugar is used and beaten with the egg whites from the start, taking about 15 minutes in a mixer.

To make Italian meringue, the sugar is boiled to a syrup with a few spoonfuls of water, the egg whites are beaten over hot water until stiff and the hot syrup is gradually poured onto the whites, whisking continuously until the mixture is stiff and glossy, then beaten again until it cools a little.

The egg whites should be at room temperature for maximum volume and bowls, beaters and other implements should be completely free of any trace of oil or fat that would prevent the expansion of the egg whites.

BASIC MERINGUE RECIPE
MAKES 8–12 MERINGUES

- 3 egg whites
- 175 g/6 oz/³⁄₄ cup caster sugar
- pinch of cream of tartar or salt

Prepare 2 baking sheets lined with non-stick baking parchment or 'Magic' baking sheet. Heat the oven to 110°C/225°F/Gas ¼.

Beat the egg whites with the cream of tartar until they form stiff peaks when the beaters are lifted, then, while continuing to beat, gradually sprinkle in about one-third of the sugar. Fold in the remaining sugar in 2 or 3 lots, cutting and folding it in gently with a large metal spoon and continuing to beat between each addition. When all the sugar has been added, shape the meringue into ovals using a tablespoon, and place these well apart on the baking sheet, as they will spread somewhat while cooking. The meringue can be piped on if preferred.

Place the baking sheet in the centre of the oven and allow the meringues to dry thoroughly for about 1–1½ hours until crisp and delicately coloured. Leave to cool in the turned-off oven, then sandwich together with lightly sweetened whipped cream. Pile them into a pyramid on a glass or china dish. They can be decorated with rose petals and strawberries, or leaves of lemon balm or scented geranium.

MERINGUE NESTS
MAKES 8–10 NESTS

This method makes a hard type of meringue suitable for nests or baskets. These are very useful to have on hand, especially in the berry season or at Christmas, and can be stored for 2–3 weeks in an airtight tin.

- 4 egg whites
- 240 g/8½ oz/1⅓ cups icing sugar (confectioner's sugar)
- ½ teaspoon vanilla extract or 2 teaspoons lemon juice

Heat the oven to 110°C/225°F/Gas ¼. Line 2 baking sheets with non-stick baking parchment or 'Magic' baking sheets.

Put the egg whites and sieved sugar into the bowl of an electric mixer. Using the whipping attachment, start beating the mixture at a slow speed until the sugar is well mixed into the whites. Turn the speed to maximum and whip until the mixture is doubled in volume, shiny and very stiff. This can take as long as 15 minutes so don't despair if nothing much seems to happen for the first 8–10 minutes. Beat in the vanilla extract or lemon juice.

If a hand-held beater is used, set the bowl over warm water and beat for 6–8 minutes or a little longer if you can. The warmth will help the mixture to increase in volume.

Using an icing bag fitted with a rose nozzle, pipe 5 rings on each sheet, starting in the centre and working out to about

7.5 cm/3 inches in diameter. Pipe another circle on top of the outside edges to make walls. Space the baskets well apart on the baking sheets. Bake in the centre of the oven on two shelves until the outsides are set and tinged a pale biscuit shade. This will take about an hour or a little longer. Turn off the heat, leaving the meringues in the oven until the oven is cool. When cold, the nests can be stored in an airtight tin for 2–3 weeks.

The nests can be filled with berries and whipped cream, ice cream and Melba sauce, sweetened chestnut purée topped with whipped cream, or whatever is available.

PAVLOVA

This well-known dessert is thought to have been created for the famous Russian ballerina Anna Pavlova, who toured Australia in 1928, although the first printed recipe had appeared in New Zealand a year earlier.

- 3 large egg whites
- 175 g/6 oz/¾ cup caster sugar
- 1 level tablespoon cornflour
- 2 teaspoons white wine or cider vinegar
- 1 teaspoon vanilla or almond extract

Line a baking sheet with non-stick baking parchment. Heat the oven to 130°C/250°F/Gas ½.

Put the egg whites into a large, perfectly clean mixing bowl. Whisk until the mixture forms stiff peaks and, while continuing to beat, gradually sprinkle in the sugar, a tablespoon at a time, until the mixture is stiff and shiny, which should take a further 5 minutes or so. Mix in the cornflour, vinegar and vanilla extract and beat for a further few moments.

Draw a circle 20–23 cm/8–9 inches in diameter on the baking sheet. Spread a layer of meringue over the circle, spoon or pipe the remainder around the edge of the circle and place the baking sheet in the centre of the oven. The pavlova will take from 1 hour to 1¼ hours to cook, when it should be crisp on the outside with a rather creamy texture inside.

Turn off the heat and allow the pavlova to cool completely before removing from the oven to avoid cracking and sinking. Inevitably this will happen a little, but that's part of the charm. When cold, carefully peel off the paper, spread with cream, ice cream or crème fraîche and top with fresh fruit.

HAZELNUT MERINGUE GATEAU
SERVES 6

- 3 egg whites
- 200 g/70 oz/1⅓ cups icing (confectioner's) sugar
- 75 g/3 oz/¾ cup ground hazelnuts
- 300 ml/½ pint/1¼ cups cream
- 5 squares good dark chocolate
- 2 tablespoons brandy or liqueur

Heat the oven to 140°C/275°F/Gas 1. Line 1 large or 2 smaller baking sheets with non-stick baking parchment.

Put the egg whites and sifted sugar into the clean bowl of a mixer and beat slowly to amalgamate the whites and sugar, then beat at high speed for about 10–15 minutes until stiff, dry peaks are formed. Fold in 2 tablespoons of the ground hazelnuts.

Mark out two 20 cm/8 inch circles on the baking sheet, divide the meringue between the circles and spread out evenly. Bake for 45–50 minutes until the meringues are crisp to the touch. Turn off the heat and allow them to cool in the oven. Peel off the paper when they are quite cold.

Fold the remaining hazelnuts into the whipped cream and use half to sandwich the meringue layers together. Spread the rest of the cream over the top. Gently melt the chocolate in the brandy over hot water and drizzle over the top of the cake. Chill for 1 hour before serving.

ANGEL CAKE

SERVES 6–8

Angel Cake is one of the glories of the American baking tradition. To bake this lightest and whitest of cakes, a special cake tin is used which is at least 15 cm/6 inches deep, with a central tube and, as with the bowl for beating egg whites, if the least trace of oil adheres to the tin, the cake will not rise. An ordinary 25 cm/10 inch spring form tin with a central tube can be pressed into service. Any excess batter can be baked separately.

- ■ pinch of salt
- ■ 275 g/10 oz/1¼ cups caster sugar
- ■ 100 g/4 oz/1 generous cup plain flour
- ■ 11 egg whites
- ■ 1 teaspoon cream of tartar (Bextartar)
- ■ 1 tablespoon lemon juice
- ■ ½ teaspoon vanilla extract

Heat the oven to 170C/325°F/Gas 3.

Add the salt and a quarter of the sugar to the flour and sift four times to incorporate as much air as possible. Sift another quarter of the sugar four times also.

Whip the egg whites until foamy and sift in the cream of tartar. Continue to beat the whites for several minutes until stiff peaks have formed. The whites should be beaten so stiffly that if 2 whole eggs are placed on top of the foam, they won't sink — an old but very effective test. Gradually beat in, a tablespoon at a time, the sifted quarter of the sugar.

Now sift a quarter of the remaining flour and sugar mixture over the batter and fold in gently and quickly with a large metal spoon. Repeat until all the flour/sugar mixture is used and finally fold in the lemon juice and vanilla. Pour the batter into the un-greased tube tin and bake in the centre of the oven for about 45 minutes. Test with a skewer.

Remove the cake from the oven, turn the cake tin upside down and rest it on the funnel, propping it up if the funnel is not high enough to keep the cake above the table surface. Leave in this position until the cake is cold, when in theory it should slide out of the tin of its own accord, though it usually needs a little urging. When quite cold, cover with plain white icing flavoured with lemon rind or vanilla. It can be served as it is or with fresh fruit.

It is difficult to cut a fresh angel cake with a knife — it is usually pried apart with two forks.

SPONGE CAKE
SERVES 6

This simple sponge cake can be whipped up in minutes and can't fail as long as the air is kept in the egg whites by the careful 'folding in' of the flour. Light and summery, the sponge can be filled with anything you fancy or used to make a simple banana pudding: layer the cake with custard (page 105) and 6 sliced bananas, cover with baking paper or foil and bake for 30 minutes. Children love it.

- 4 eggs
- 100 g/4 oz/½ cup caster sugar
- 100 g/4 oz/1 cup plus 2 tablespoons sifted flour
- vanilla extract or lemon juice
- 6 oz whipped cream and raspberry jam, for filling
- icing sugar, for dusting

Line two 20 cm/8 inch sandwich tins with baking parchment or butter them well and sprinkle with sugar, shaking out any excess. Heat the oven to 190°C/375°F/Gas 5.

Put the eggs and sugar in a large bowl and beat until the mixture is pale, thick and creamy and retains a 'trail' when the beaters are lifted, then beat in the vanilla extract and lemon juice. With a large metal spoon, fold in the sifted flour in 3 lots, cutting in the flour with the side of the spoon and folding the mixture over rather than stirring, which forces the air out. Try to do this with the minimum of cutting and folding, but without leaving lumps of flour in the mixture.

Divide the mixture between the tins, level the top lightly and bake in the centre of the oven on two shelves for 9–12 minutes until the cakes are just beginning to shrink away from the sides of the tins.

Turn the cakes upside down onto a wire rack and allow to cool completely. Fill with whipped cream and raspberry jam and sieve a little icing sugar over the top. A layer of crushed strawberries or raspberries spread between the jam and cream is rather good, too.

LEMON TORTE
SERVES 6

Margaret Costa, the food writer, once memorably wrote that the only sort of cake worth putting on weight for was one made with ground almonds! This moist and buttery cake with the sharp tang of lemons is adapted from an eighteenth-century recipe when ground almonds were often used instead of flour.

- ■ 2 lemons
- ■ 175 g/6 oz/¾ cup butter
- ■ 175 g/6 oz/¾ cup caster sugar
- ■ 5 egg yolks
- ■ 3 egg whites
- ■ 100 g/4 oz/1 cup ground almonds
- ■ a few drops of almond extract
- ■ 1 tablespoon icing sugar and 2 tablespoons flaked almonds, for decoration

Heat the oven to 180°C/350°F/Gas 4. Line a 20 cm/8 inch square cake tin with non-stick baking parchment.

Grate the lemons and squeeze out the juice. If the lemons are very large and juicy, omit the juice of half a lemon.

Put the softened butter, sugar, egg yolks and egg whites, lemon rind and juice in a large bowl and beat well for 3 or 4 minutes until the mixture is light and creamy. Fold in the ground almonds and add 1 or 2 drops of almond extract. Pour into the prepared tin and bake in the centre of the oven for about 40 minutes until the cake has shrunk slightly from the sides of the tin.

Allow the cake to cool in the tin before turning out carefully as it is rather fragile. Before serving, scatter toasted almond flakes over the top and dust with the icing sugar rubbed through a sieve.

This is a rather rich cake and will serve at least 6 for dessert. A spoonful or two of lemon curd beaten into some whipped crème fraîche is delicious on the side.

WALNUT LAYER CAKE
SERVES 8

This adaptation of a Viennese classic is elegant enough for a dinner party dessert with the great advantage that it can be made at least a day in advance.

Cake

- 65 g/2½ oz/½ cup very finely chopped walnuts
- 6 eggs
- 175 g/6 oz/¾ cup golden caster sugar
- ¼ teaspoon baking powder
- 1 tablespoon fine white breadcrumbs
- a few walnut halves, for decoration

Butter cream

- 100 g/4 oz/8 squares good dark chocolate
- 2 tablespoons brown rum, brandy or other liqueur
- 225 g/8 oz/1 cup unsalted butter
- 1 egg
- 150 g/5 oz/8 tablespoons icing sugar
- a pinch of ground cloves

Line three 20 cm/8 inch sandwich tins with non-stick baking parchment. Preheat the oven to 180°C/350°F/Gas 4.

Chop the nuts in a small electric chopper until they resemble fine breadcrumbs, pulsing for a few seconds at a time and being careful not to grind them into a paste, or chop them very finely by hand with a good sharp knife.

Put the eggs with the sugar in a mixing bowl and whip at full speed until the mixture is thick, pale and creamy. Mix the baking powder, breadcrumbs and nuts together and, using a large metal spoon, fold lightly and evenly into the egg mixture. Divide between the 3 lined cake tins and bake on three shelves, in rotation if necessary, for 12–14 minutes. Remove from the oven, allow to cool for a few moments before carefully turning out these rather fragile cakes onto wire racks previously lined with baking paper or foil.

To make the butter cream, melt the chocolate with the rum, using the defrost setting on the microwave and giving it several 30 second bursts, with standing time between, until the chocolate has softened. Rest until ready to use. (The chocolate can also be melted over hot water.)

Put the softened butter in a mixing bowl with the egg and beat until creamy. Add the icing sugar, cloves and a tablespoon of boiling water. Beat on full speed until the mixture is light and fluffy. Beat in the melted chocolate and whip again until the chocolate is completely amalgamated. Use half the mixture to spread between the cake layers, using the remainder for the top and sides. Decorate with the reserved walnut halves. Cover with foil and store in the fridge until required.

8
Custards

Custards in their various forms are among the earliest of simple sweet dishes. The Romans have left recipes for them which were highly flavoured and baked in earthen dishes. Nearer home, our medieval ancestors baked them in pastry 'coffins' or boiled them tied up in cloths like Christmas puddings. They held the egg yolk in much higher regard than the white — custards made for 'lords' used only yolks, while those for ordinary folk used the whole egg.

This basic custard recipe, which has changed surprisingly little from those times, can be used with puddings or trifles or as a base for ice cream. Enriched with melted chocolate it makes an excellent sauce. For a richer custard replace the milk with cream.

BASIC CUSTARD

SERVES 6

- 1 vanilla pod or ½ teaspoon vanilla extract
- 300 ml/½ pint/1¼ cups milk
- 300 ml/½ pint/1¼ cups cream
- 6 egg yolks
- 1 good teaspoon cornflour
- 40 g/1½ oz/3 tablespoons caster sugar

Split the vanilla pod lengthways and scrape out the sticky seeds. Put these and the pod or extract into a saucepan with the milk and cream. Heat slowly almost to the boil, remove from the heat and leave to infuse for 10 minutes before removing the pod. The pod can be rinsed, dried and stored in a jar of caster sugar kept for baking.

Beat the egg yolks, cornflour and sugar together until pale and creamy. Pour the cream/milk mixture slowly onto the eggs, beating well while pouring. Return the custard to the saucepan and reheat, stirring continually until the mixture coats the back of a spoon and leaves a clear space when a finger is run through the coating. Be careful, of course, not to let it boil. Allow the custard to cool, stirring from time to time to prevent a skin forming. Cover with clingfilm and keep in the fridge until ready to use.

PASTRY CREAM (CRÈME PÂTISSIÈRE)
MAKES 6 TARTLETS

This cream can be used alone or mixed with whipped cream for cake fillings. It is also used to provide a base for the fruit when making fresh fruit tarlets or flans.

- 3 egg yolks
- 75 g/3 oz/6 tablespoons caster sugar
- 40 g/1½ oz/3 tablespoons flour
- 300 ml/½ pint/1¼ cups milk

Put the yolks, sugar and flour in a bowl and beat well together. Bring the milk to the boil and pour slowly onto the eggs, beating well. Return the mixture to the saucepan and simmer slowly for 3–4 minutes, stirring continuously. This pastry cream is quite thick. Add a little more hot milk if a more fluid mixture is called for. Cover and chill until required.

CRÈME BRÛLÉE
SERVES 6

Although this delicious cream has its origins in France, it has been a popular dish in Scotland since the eighteenth century, appearing in 1759 in Mrs Elizabeth Cleland's *A New and Easy Method of Cookery* under the guise of 'A Burnt Cream'.

- 1 vanilla pod or ½ teaspoon vanilla extract
- 600 ml/1 pint/3 cups cream
- 6 egg yolks
- 50 g/2 oz/4 level tablespoons caster sugar

You will need 6 ramekins or 1 larger oven dish. Heat the oven to 140°C/275°F/Gas 1.

Split the vanilla pod lengthways and scrape out the sticky seeds. Put these with the pod or extract into a saucepan with the cream. Bring almost to the boil, then leave to infuse for 10 minutes before removing the pod. The pod can be rinsed and dried and stored in a jar of sugar for future use.

Beat the egg yolks and half the sugar until thick and creamy. Reheat the cream to just below boiling point and pour onto the yolks, continuing to beat as you pour. Return the mixture to the saucepan and cook over a low heat, stirring all the time, until the mixture coats the back of the spoon and is beginning to thicken slightly around the tip of the spoon, but don't allow it to boil.

Set the ramekins in a roasting tin and divide the custard between them. Pour enough warm water into the tin to come two-thirds of the way up the sides of the dishes, lay a sheet of foil over the top and bake in the centre of the oven until the custard is set (about 40 minutes for the smaller dishes, 50 minutes for a large dish). Remove from the oven. If not quite set, leave the dishes in the water until cool. Chill for a few hours or overnight.

Heat the grill. Use the remaining 2 tablespoons of sugar to lightly dust the surface of the creams, spreading it as evenly as possible. Slide the dishes under the hot grill and let the sugar melt to a good golden brown. Stand in a cool spot for 1 hour or so until the sugar sets to a nice hard shell.

Fresh fruit is often served with Crème Brûlée. Raspberries make a particularly good partnership.

CRÈME CARAMEL
SERVES 6

Caramel

- 100 g/4 oz/5 heaped tablespoons granulated sugar
- 3 tablespoons water

Custard

- 300 ml/½ pint/1¼ cups milk
- 300 ml/½ pint/1¼ cups cream
- 25 g/1 oz/2 tablespoons caster sugar
- vanilla pod or ½ teaspoon vanilla extract
- 2 whole eggs
- 3 egg yolks

You will need 6 ramekins or 1 large 1–1.5 litre/1½–2 pint oven dish. Set the oven at 140°C/275°F/Gas 1.

To make the caramel, put the sugar in a small saucepan with the water. Stir over a low heat until the sugar has dissolved completely before allowing it to boil. Boil without stirring until the sugar is a rich brown colour, watching carefully, however, as sugar can burn very quickly once it starts to brown. Pour at once into the heated dishes and leave until it sets hard.

While the caramel is setting, put the milk, cream, sugar and the vanilla pod or extract in a saucepan and bring almost to the boil. Remove from the heat and allow the vanilla to infuse until the liquid is cool. Remove the vanilla pod, which can be washed, dried and stored in a jar of sugar.

Beat the whole eggs and yolks lightly together with a whisk. Pour the milk and cream mixture onto the eggs, mixing thoroughly together, then pour the mixture through a sieve into a jug. Set the ramekins in a roasting tin and divide the custard between them. Add warm water to the tin to come two-thirds of the way up the sides of the dishes. Cover with tin foil and bake in the centre of the oven for 50–60 minutes. If using one large dish, it may take another 10 minutes or so.

Carefully lift the tin from the oven. If the custards are still a little wobbly, leave them in the hot water until cool.

The Crème Caramel is ready to eat after a few hours' chilling. If it can be made a day ahead, however, the caramel will have time to dissolve, giving a delicious sauce.

To turn out, run a thin knife around the insides of the dishes and upend onto a deep serving plate. A little whipped cream or crème fraîche can be served on the side.

ZABAGLIONE
SERVES 2–3

This lovely Italian dessert is served in small glasses with sponge fingers or slices of plain cake. It can also be used to top fresh fruit and flashed briefly under a hot grill.

- 6 egg yolks
- 40 g/1½ oz/3 tablespoons caster sugar
- 150 ml/¼ pint/⅝ cup Marsala or similar sweet wine

Choose a large bowl that will fit over a saucepan or use a double boiler, and put in the egg yolks and sugar. First whip the mixture with a balloon whisk or an electric beater until it is pale and beginning to foam, then set the bowl over hot water and keep whisking hard until the volume has increased and the mixture has begun to thicken. Start adding the Marsala a little at a time, whisking until all the wine has been added and the mixture is light, foamy and doubled in volume.

All this beating takes a little energy, but it can't go wrong and the taste is heavenly. Serve immediately.

STRAWBERRY ICE CREAM
SERVES 6

For those of us who don't own an ice cream maker, a rich custard base helps prevent the formation of ice crystals and makes a good smooth ice cream with the minimum of mixing and beating.

- 6 egg yolks
- 150 g/5 oz/⅔ cup caster sugar
- 150 ml/¼ pint/⅝ cup milk
- 600 ml/1 pint/3 cups cream
- 350 g/12 oz/2½ cups strawberries, puréed

You will need a 1½ litre/2 pint plastic box or loaf tin.

Beat the egg yolks with the sugar until thick and creamy. Bring the milk and cream to the boil, then pour gradually onto the eggs, mixing well while pouring. Return the mixture to the saucepan and stir over a low heat until it thickens slightly and coats the back of a spoon, leaving a distinct trail when a finger is run through the coating, but don't let it boil. Allow the mixture to cool completely before folding in the strawberries.

Pour into the container. Freeze for about 1 hour. Remove from the freezer and beat well with a fork, scraping the frozen mixture from the bottom and sides into the centre before returning to the freezer. This initial beating can be done in a processor or blender, if preferred. Repeat this process once or twice more until the ice cream is frozen (5–6 hours). Allow to defrost at room temperature for 20 minutes before serving.

Note: The strawberry purée can be replaced by the same quantity of other fruit purées such as raspberry, peach, etc.

BAKED LEMON CHEESECAKE
SERVES 6

- 250 g/9 oz ginger snap or digestive biscuits
- 150 g/5 oz/⅝ cup butter
- 6 large eggs
- 375 g/14 oz/2¼ cups ricotta or Philadelphia cream cheese
- 375 g/14 oz/2¼ cups Mascarpone cheese
- 150 ml/¼ pint/⅝ cup sour or double cream
- rind of 2 medium lemons
- 175 g/6 oz/¾ cup golden caster sugar
- 4 tablespoons cornflour
- salt

Line a 24 cm/9–10 inch spring form tin with baking parchment and butter well. Heat the oven to150°C/300°F/Gas 2.

Crush the biscuits with a rolling pin or use a food processor, stir in the melted butter and mix together. Spread evenly over the base of the tin and press down firmly with the bottom of a bottle. Chill in the fridge until set.

Put the eggs, cheeses, sour cream and lemon rind into a large mixer bowl. Mix the sugar and cornflour together with a pinch of salt and sift through a sieve over the contents of the bowl. Turn on the mixer at a slow speed until the cornflour is well mixed in, then beat at high speed for 10 minutes until the mixture is light, fluffy and creamy. Pour into the prepared tin and bake in the centre of the oven for 1¼ hours. Don't open the oven while the cake is baking. Turn off the heat, leaving the cake in the oven for about 2 hours without opening the door, then remove and chill until required.

Carefully remove the spring form tin and slide the cake gently onto a serving dish. Cover with strawberries or other seasonal fruit, dust with icing sugar and serve.

Note: If a mixer is unavailable, work the cheeses through a sieve. Separate the eggs, beating the whites to soft peaks and folding in finally when the other ingredients have been well beaten together.

QUEEN OF PUDDINGS
SERVES 6

A light and elegant version of this homely pudding. When raspberries are in season it can be dressed up with a raspberry sauce or a layer of raspberries underneath the meringue.

- 5 eggs
- 300 ml/½ pint/1¼ cups cream
- 1 teaspoon vanilla essence
- grated lemon rind
- 400 ml/¾ pint/2 cups milk
- 2 tablespoons caster sugar for the pudding
- 75 g/3 oz/1 cup fine white breadcrumbs
- 4–5 tablespoons raspberry jam
- 150 g/5 oz/⅔ cup caster sugar for the meringue

Separate 3 of the eggs and set the whites aside for the meringue. Beat together the remaining eggs, yolks, cream, flavourings, milk and the 2 tablespoons of sugar. Put the breadcrumbs in an ovenproof dish, pour the cream and egg mixture over them and leave to infuse for 1 hour or longer if time allows.

Heat the oven to 160°C/325°F/Gas 3. Bake the crumb and custard mixture in the centre of the oven for 15–20 minutes until set. Allow it to cool for a few minutes, then spread the jam evenly over the surface.

Raise the oven temperature to 190°C/375°F/Gas 5. Beat the egg whites until they form stiff peaks. Slowly sprinkle in 75 g/3 oz/⅓ cup of the sugar, whisking continuously. Using a large metal spoon, fold in the remaining sugar thoroughly. Spread the meringue evenly over the jam, fluffing it up a little to make peaks, and bake for 15 minutes until the meringue is set and lightly browned, keeping an eye on it as it can burn easily. Allow it to cool a little before serving with a little whipped cream or crème fraîche.

9
Sauces

In this small selection of egg and flour-based sauces the Fresh Tomato Sauce and the Spicy Vinaigrette may seem the odd men out. However, the Fresh Tomato Sauce harmonises so well with many egg dishes, notably Omelettes and Soufflés, and the Spicy Vinaigrette is so universally useful that they have earned their place.

SAUCE HOLLANDAISE
SERVES 6–8

Despite its name, Sauce Hollandaise is one of France's most important sauces, providing a luxurious partner for fish, eggs and vegetable dishes. It's easy to make, keeping in mind, as with custards, that the egg yolks will scramble if the heat is too great. Make the sauce in a double saucepan or a bowl over hot, not boiling, water.

- 3 tablespoons white wine vinegar or 4 tablespoons dry white wine
- 1 teaspoon peppercorns
- 3 tablespoons water
- 5 egg yolks
- 175 g/6 oz/¾ cup unsalted butter, melted
- lemon juice
- salt

Put the wine, peppercorns and the 3 tablespoons of water in a small saucepan and reduce to 1 tablespoon. Pour this reduction through a sieve into the bowl set over hot water. Add the egg yolks and a few drops of water and mix well together with a small whisk or wooden spoon, stirring continually until the yolks begin to thicken slightly.

Now start adding the tepid melted butter, a little at a time, working the butter in well before the next addition and checking that the water in the saucepan is not boiling. Continue stirring until the eggs begin to emulsify and the sauce is smooth and begins to thicken — this can take 10 minutes or more. Finally, add a little lemon juice to taste. (If salted butter is used, it probably won't need salt.) The sauce is served warm and it will thicken further as it cools. To keep it warm, leave the bowl over warm water and press clingfilm flat on the surface to prevent a skin forming.

To rescue Hollandaise on the verge of scrambling, try a speedy transfer of the mixture to a mini-chopper or blender (the quantity is too small to work in a food processor) and whiz vigorously. The result will be a slightly foamy aerated sauce that can be held for several hours or overnight in the fridge. This is no longer true Hollandaise, of course, but truly delicious nevertheless.

SAUCE BÉARNAISE
SERVES 6–8

Béarnaise uses the same method and ingredients as Hollandaise but with a differently flavoured base, and it is so delicious that my loved ones have invented the Béarnaise Butty, a hamburger bun filled with leftover Béarnaise, a rare enough treat as there is seldom any left.

- 2 tablespoons fresh tarragon, finely chopped or ½ teaspoon dried tarragon
- 3 tablespoons white wine vinegar or 4 tablespoons white wine
- 1 tablespoon chives, finely chopped
- 40 g/1½ oz/½ cup shallots or onions, finely chopped
- ¼ teaspoon white peppercorns
- 3 tablespoons cold water
- 5 egg yolks
- 1 tablespoon water
- 175 g/6 oz/¾ cup butter, melted
- lemon juice
- sea salt and freshly ground white pepper

Reserve a few leaves of tarragon for decoration and put the remainder in a saucepan with the vinegar, chives, shallots, peppercorns and water and simmer over a low heat until reduced by half. Strain this liquid into a bowl placed over hot water and continue as for Hollandaise, using the same quantity of eggs and butter.

Place a few tarragon leaves on top of the finished sauce when serving.

BÉCHAMEL SAUCE
SERVES 6–8

Béchamel is perhaps the most useful of all the flour sauces as it forms the basis of so many others. Follow the steps to achieve a smooth silky texture and a good flavour.

- 600 ml/1 pint/3 cups milk
- ½ small onion
- ¼ carrot, chopped
- nutmeg
- 1 bay leaf
- 3 cloves
- 50 g/2 oz/4 tablespoons butter
- 50 g/2 oz/⅓ cup flour
- salt and black pepper

Put the milk, onion, carrot, a pinch of nutmeg, bay leaf, seasoning and cloves in a small saucepan and slowly bring to the boil, simmering gently for about 5 minutes. Turn off the heat and allow the milk to infuse for 10 minutes, then strain and keep warm.

In a small heavy saucepan melt the butter over a low heat and mix in the flour. Stir this well for 2–3 minutes with a wooden spoon, but don't let it brown. Take the pan off the heat and gradually work in the warm milk, a little at a time, whisking in each addition until it's smooth before adding the next. Return to the heat and bring the sauce back to a gentle simmer, stirring all the time until smooth and shiny.

Now turn the heat as low as possible and allow the sauce to cook for 6–7 minutes, stirring from time to time and making sure it doesn't burn. This slow cooking of the flour is important and avoids that pasty flavour which has given this type of sauce such a bad reputation.

Check the seasoning and the sauce is ready. If it needs to be kept warm or reheated, set the saucepan in a larger one containing hot water. To prevent a skin forming, either lay a piece of clingfilm directly on the surface or dot with tiny pieces of butter to form a film on top.

SAUCE AURORE

SERVES 6–8

- 75 ml/3 fl oz/⅓ cup double cream
- ½ quantity Béchamel Sauce (page 119)
- 100 ml/4 fl oz/½ cup Fresh Tomato Sauce (page 122)
- 15 g/½ oz/1 tablespoon butter
- salt and black pepper

Blend the cream and Béchamel sauce together in a medium saucepan and bring to just below boiling point, stirring well. Add tomato sauce and seasoning to taste and simmer gently for 3 or 4 minutes. Finally, whisk in the cold butter in little pieces and serve.

SAUCE MORNAY
SERVES 6–8

Sauce Mornay is the ideal sauce for gratins of all kinds. For a less rich sauce leave out the eggs. Strong Cheddar can be used instead of the Parmesan and Gruyère, adding an extra tablespoon or so for a good flavour.

- 2 egg yolks
- 50 ml/2 fl oz/¼ cup double cream
- ½ quantity Béchamel Sauce (page 119)
- 2 large tablespoons each of grated Parmesan and Gruyère
- salt and black pepper

Beat the egg yolks into the cream. Bring the Béchamel almost to boiling point and simmer for 2–3 minutes. Whisk the eggs and cream mixture into the Béchamel, allow it to just barely bubble up for a moment and immediately take it off the heat.

Mix in the finely grated cheese and keep stirring until the cheese has melted. Season well and the sauce is ready to serve. It can be reheated gently over hot water, keeping in mind that too much heat will make the cheese stringy.

FRESH TOMATO SAUCE
SERVES 6–8

- 1 medium onion, finely chopped
- 15 g/½ oz/1 tablespoon butter
- 1 tablespoon olive oil
- 8 large ripe tomatoes, coarsely chopped
- 1 tablespoon basil leaves or 1 bay leaf
- 1 teaspoon sugar
- 1 teaspoon salt
- ¼ teaspoon cayenne pepper

Sauté the onion in the butter and olive oil, without allowing it to brown, until soft. Add the tomatoes, herbs and seasoning and cook slowly for 20–25 minutes. If the sauce seems too liquid, reduce it by cooking a little while longer. Check the seasoning.

Transfer the sauce to a blender or food processor and whiz to a smooth purée. If you prefer a finer finish, push the mixture through a sieve to remove the seeds and skins.

The sauce will keep for 3–4 days, covered, in the fridge.

SPICY VINAIGRETTE
SERVES 6–8

- ½ medium red pepper
- 1–2 shallots or ½ small onion
- 1–2 tablespoons fresh coriander or basil
- 1 small red chilli, seeded and finely chopped

- juice of 1 lime
- small tablespoon balsamic vinegar
- 5–6 tablespoons vegetable or mild olive oil, or mixture of both
- salt and cayenne pepper

Put the red pepper, skin side up, under a hot grill until the skin begins to blacken and blister. Wrap loosely in foil until cool enough to remove the skin. Chop as finely as possible. Slice the shallots and chop finely. Wash the herbs, pat dry in kitchen paper and chop coarsely. Add to the remaining ingredients and leave to infuse until required.

MAYONNAISE
SERVES 6–8

Mayonnaise and its near relations are simple emulsions of eggs and oil and, in some cases, cream. These sauces are not difficult to make if a few ground rules are followed, and by changing the flavourings a whole range of sauces is at your disposal. They do, however, contain raw eggs and vulnerable people may prefer to avoid them or use the Herb and Egg Sauce on page 128 instead which uses hard-boiled eggs.

Olive oil is the obvious choice but if yours is a rich, green, fruity one, then groundnut or sunflower oil should compose the greater part of the total, with the olive oil making up about a quarter, as it tends to overpower the flavour of the food. A few spoonfuls of walnut oil, used in place of olive oil, gives an excellent sauce for shellfish, especially lobster.

No special equipment is needed, just a small bowl with a damp cloth underneath to stop it sliding about. You will also need a wooden spoon or wire whisk or use a hand-held mixer at medium speed. I have seen wonderful mayonnaise made on a plate, using two forks, but I haven't had any success with this method myself.

Excellent mayonnaise can be made in a blender, using whole eggs and adding the oil after the initial stage in a thin steady stream. It is undeniably fast, but there is a simple pleasure in making mayonnaise by hand and seeing such basic ingredients slowly turn into that magical golden emulsion.

There are divided opinions concerning the temperature of the eggs (whether room or fridge temperature is best). I find it doesn't make much difference. The oil is best at room temperature, however, so if it has congealed in cold weather, stand the bottle in warm water until it is clear again.

- 3 egg yolks*
- 2 teaspoons Dijon mustard
- 300 ml/½ pint/1¼ cups oil
- lemon juice or white wine vinegar
- salt and white pepper

Put the egg yolks and mustard in a heavy bowl, add a pinch of salt and 1 or 2 twists of pepper, break up the yolks with the spoon or whisk and stir well for a few moments to amalgamate the eggs and mustard completely.

Pour the oil into a small jug with a good pouring lip and slowly, drip by drip, start adding the oil, stirring with a gentle rhythm and working in each addition before adding the next. As the emulsion thickens, the pouring can be speeded up to a thin stream. If the emulsion becomes too thick, thin it slightly from time to time with a few drops of vinegar or lemon juice. When all the oil has been added, taste for seasoning, adding more as required. The mixture should be thick and creamy.

Should the mixture separate or fail to emulsify, start again in a clean bowl with 1 egg yolk and, as before, gradually add the separated mixture, drop by drop, stirring continuously until it starts to thicken, when you can add the remainder more rapidly. A useful method when you need to make a large quantity of mayonnaise in a hurry is to start by adding 2–3 tablespoons of good quality commercial mayonnaise to the egg yolks and flavourings and work from there — the additional oil will emulsify more rapidly as it is worked in.

If you intend to use the mayonnaise the same day, it's nicer kept in a cool place, but for longer storage keep it covered in the fridge. It will keep for 2 or 3 days.

*Two egg yolks are enough to absorb 300 ml/½ pint/1¼ cups of oil, but the sauce is less likely to separate if the extra yolk is used.

AÏOLI GARLIC MAYONNAISE

- 3–4 cloves garlic
- 3–4 egg yolks
- salt
- 2 teaspoons Dijon mustard
- 300 ml/½ pint/1¼ cups oil
- lemon juice
- 1 tablespoon parsley, very finely chopped

Chop the peeled garlic roughly, then crush to a paste with the point of a knife and a little salt. Beat into the egg yolks with the mustard before starting to add the oil. Continue beating and adding the oil gradually, as in the previous recipe. Add lemon juice to taste and finish with the parsley.

SAUCE REMOULADE
SERVES 6–8

This piquant sauce is redolent of garden buffets and picnics and, for me, really makes Chef's Salad worth eating.

- 2–3 anchovies or more, to taste
- 1 quantity mayonnaise (page 123)
- 1 level tablespoon each chopped capers, gherkin, parsley and chives
- 1 teaspoon finely chopped fresh tarragon leaves

Rinse the anchovies in warm water and pat dry. Chop coarsely and beat them with the other ingredients into the mayonnaise. Check the seasoning and the sauce is ready.

RED PEPPER SAUCE
SERVES 6–8

Serve this delectable sauce with eggs, fish, vegetables or poached chicken.

- 1 medium red pepper
- 200 ml/8 fl oz/1 cup light chicken stock
- 3 egg yolks
- 50 g/2 oz/4 tablespoons butter, cubed
- salt and white pepper

Cut the pepper into quarters and remove the white pith and seeds. Flatten out the sections and spread them under a hot grill, skin side up, until the skin blisters and blackens and the pepper has softened. Wrap loosely in foil until cool enough to handle before removing the skin. Chop coarsely, put into a blender with the stock, whiz until smooth, and pour into a medium size bowl.

Set the bowl over hot water and beat in the egg yolks, using a wire whisk. Continue whisking the mixture until it thickens slightly and coats the back of a wooden spoon, then whisk in the butter, a few cubes at a time.

Taste for seasoning and the sauce is ready to serve. It can be kept warm over the hot water until required.

HERB AND EGG SAUCE

SERVES 6–8

The herbs and flavourings can be added or subtracted to taste in this easy to make sauce. It's ideal, too, for mayonnaise lovers when raw eggs are out of bounds.

- 4 hard-boiled eggs
- 1 tablespoon Dijon mustard
- 1 tablespoon cider or white wine vinegar
- 200 ml/8 fl oz/1 cup sunflower or bland olive oil
- 3–4 tablespoons finely chopped parsley
- 2 tablespoons finely chopped chives
- 1 teaspoon finely chopped tarragon
- 3–4 finely chopped scallions
- 1 tablespoon drained capers
- ½ red chilli, very finely chopped
- salt and black pepper

Shell the eggs, remove the yolks, put them in a bowl and crush to a smooth paste with the mustard, vinegar, salt and pepper. Work in the oil gradually as for mayonnaise, beating well with a wire whisk. Add the herbs, scallions, capers, chilli and finally the chopped egg whites. Allow to infuse for 30 minutes or so and serve.

10

A Few Soups

Here are some simple, easy-to-prepare soups, and though they require very similar ingredients (with one exception), their origins are in very different countries and give very different results.

ZUPPA ALLA PAVESI

SERVES 1

This wonderfully restorative Italian soup can be quickly put together with the simplest of ingredients. Homemade chicken stock is best, of course, but a stock cube works very well, too.

- 200 ml/8 fl oz/1 cup chicken stock
- 1 large peeled clove of garlic, crushed (optional)
- 4 small triangles of good bread
- butter and olive oil for frying the bread
- 1 tablespoon grated Parmesan or Cheddar
- 1 egg

Bring the stock to a gentle simmer with the garlic and while it is heating, fry the bread in a little butter and olive oil. Sprinkle the slices generously with the cheese and keep warm. Poach the egg in the stock, lift out with a perforated slice, trim neatly around the edges and lay in a heated soup plate. Strain the stock over the egg, float the pieces of bread on top and serve.

STRACCIATELLA

SERVES 4

A very simple recipe based on Elizabeth David's directions for this most popular of Roman soups.

- 3 eggs
- 2 tablespoons grated Parmesan
- 1 tablespoon semolina or ½ tablespoon cornflour
- 1 litre/1¾ pints/5 cups chicken stock

Put the eggs in a small bowl with the Parmesan and semolina, add a cupful of hot stock and whisk together until smooth. Bring the remaining stock almost to the boil, slowly pour in the egg mixture in a fine stream and beat it hard with a fork for 3–4 minutes. Take the saucepan off the heat and leave the soup to sit for 2 minutes — the egg mixture will have broken into fine threads. Serve immediately.

CHINESE CORN AND CRAB SOUP

SERVES 4

Finely chopped ham is sometimes used in place of the crab in this lovely soup. 150 g/5 oz/¾ cup of ham will be enough.

- 1 tablespoon cornflour
- 3 tablespoons milk
- 3 egg whites
- 900 ml/1½ pints/4¼ cups chicken stock
- 1 x 225 g/8 oz can creamed corn
- 225 g/8 oz/1½ cups cooked white crab meat
- salt

Mix the cornflour with the milk and set aside. Beat the egg whites in a small bowl until they begin to foam and then beat in 2 tablespoons of the stock. Bring the remaining stock to the boil, add the corn and the cornflour mixture, stirring well until the soup thickens slightly. Add the crab meat and bring the soup almost to the boil again before sliding the pan off the heat. Immediately pour in the egg white mixture. Add salt to taste. Stir just once and leave to sit for 1 minute before serving.

CHICKEN SOUP WITH WRAPPED SAVOURY CUSTARD

SERVES 4

Another oriental adaptation, this time from Japan, where the stock used is dashi, a delicately flavoured stock made from bonito flakes and kombu (kelp), which can be bought in instant form in oriental grocers. In *this* recipe a light homemade chicken stock is used, and the soup can be served hot or cold. Serve in small glasses or porcelain bowls.

Egg mixture

- ¼ red pepper
- 2 tablespoons tiny peas or 6 fine green beans
- 100 g/4 oz/¾ cup cooked prawns
- 4 eggs

Soup

- 900 ml/1½ pints/4¼ cups chicken stock or dashi
- 2 tablespoons sake or dry sherry
- ½ tablespoon Kikkoman soy sauce
- 2.5 cm/1 inch piece fresh ginger
- 1½ level tablespoons cornflour
- 2 tablespoons water
- parsley
- salt

Put the stock, sherry, soy sauce and the grated ginger in a saucepan and simmer gently for 5 minutes. Leave to infuse while preparing the eggs.

Cut the red pepper (and beans, if they are used) into very fine strips about 2.5 cm/1 inch long and blanch with the peas in boiling water for 1 minute, then plunge the vegetables into cold water to cool. Drain well.

Line 4 small teacups with clingfilm, leaving a generous overhang. Divide the vegetables and prawns between the cups and pour in the beaten eggs. Season to taste. Gather up the clingfilm edges, twist firmly and tie very tightly with string, making little pouches. Bring a pot of water to the boil, lower the heat and drop in the pouches, poaching gently with the water just below boiling for 9–10 minutes until the custards are set. Remove from the water and when cool enough to handle, unwrap the custards and place one in each bowl.

Strain the stock, return it to the saucepan and bring to a gentle simmer. Add the cornflour previously blended with the 2 tablespoons of water and stir well until the stock is clear and slightly thickened. Taste for seasoning. Pour the stock over the custards and serve garnished with a little parsley.

BORSCHT WITH HARD-BOILED EGGS
SERVES 4–5

Made in a blender, this almost instant borscht is garnished with hard-boiled eggs, sour cream and dill and it's equally good hot or cold, depending on the weather. Cooked baby beetroot, vacuum-packed, 4 or 5 to a pack and available in most supermarkets, is used here. Freshly cooked beets or jars of very lightly pickled beets can also be used.

- 1 packet (5 baby beets) cooked beetroot
- 1 small red onion
- 1 or 2 cloves garlic, finely chopped
- 1 seeded red chilli or cayenne pepper to taste
- 3–5 pickled gherkins
- 750 ml/1¼ pints/3½ cups good tomato juice
- 300 ml/½ pint/1¼ cups chicken stock
- 1 tablespoon sour cream or crème fraîche per person
- 1 hard-boiled egg per person
- 2 tablespoons finely chopped dill or coriander
- salt and black pepper

Roughly chop the beetroot and peeled onion and put in a blender with the garlic, chilli, gherkins and half the tomato juice. Blend until the mixture is smooth, pour into a large saucepan, add the chicken stock and enough of the remaining tomato juice to give the consistency you like. Season to taste. If you are serving the soup cold, season it very generously as the cold diminishes the flavour and it really should be quite spicy. If it's to be served hot, bring it to a gentle simmer for 5 minutes or so.

Divide the soup between the dishes, float a tablespoon of cream on each, arrange a sliced egg on top and sprinkle with the dill.

Note: Some brands of pickled beetroot are prepared in rather savage vinegar. If this is the case, rinse the beets thoroughly before blending. The proportion of beetroot to tomato juice can be adjusted to taste.

Index